150 MOST FAMOUS *Poems*

POETRY HOUSE

ISBN: 978-1-64-775107-4

"

Poetry is the journal of the sea animal living on land, wanting to fly in the air. Poetry is a search for syllables to shoot at the barriers of the unknown and the unknowable. Poetry is a phantom script telling how rainbows are made and why they go away.

CARL SANDBURG

TABLE OF CONTENTS

viii

DOVER BEACH

by Matthew Arnold

The sea is calm tonight.
The tide is full, the moon lies fair
Upon the straits; on the French coast, the light
Gleams and is gone; the cliffs of England stand,
Glimmering and vast, out in the tranquil bay.
Come to the window, sweet is the night-air!
Only, from the long line of spray
Where the sea meets the moon-blanched land,
Listen! you hear the grating roar
Of pebbles which the waves draw back, and fling,
At their return, up the high strand,
Begin, and cease, and then again begin,
With tremulous cadence slow, and bring
The eternal note of sadness in.
Sophocles long ago
Heard it on the Aegean, and it brought
Into his mind the turbid ebb and flow
Of human misery; we
Find also in the sound a thought,
Hearing it by this distant northern sea.
The Sea of Faith
Was once, too, at the full, and round earth's shore
Lay like the folds of a bright girdle furled.
But now I only hear
Its melancholy, long, withdrawing roar,
Retreating, to the breath
Of the night-wind, down the vast edges drear

And naked shingles of the world.
Ah, love, let us be true
To one another! for the world, which seems
To lie before us like a land of dreams,
So various, so beautiful, so new,
Hath really neither joy, nor love, nor light,
Nor certitude, nor peace, nor help for pain;
And we are here as on a darkling plain
Swept with confused alarms of struggle and flight,
Where ignorant armies clash by night.

AUGURIES OF INNOCENCE
by William Blake

To see a world in a grain of sand,
    And a heaven in a wild flower,
Hold infinity in the palm of your hand,
    And eternity in an hour.

A robin redbreast in a cage
Puts all heaven in a rage.
A dove-house fill'd with doves and pigeons
Shudders hell thro' all its regions.
A dog starv'd at his master's gate
Predicts the ruin of the state.
A horse misused upon the road
Calls to heaven for human blood.
Each outcry of the hunted hare
A fibre from the brain does tear.
A skylark wounded in the wing,
A cherubim does cease to sing.
The game-cock clipt and arm'd for fight
Does the rising sun affright.

Every wolf's and lion's howl
Raises from hell a human soul.
The wild deer, wand'ring here and there,
Keeps the human soul from care.
The lamb misus'd breeds public strife,
And yet forgives the butcher's knife.

The bat that flits at close of eve
Has left the brain that won't believe.
The owl that calls upon the night
Speaks the unbeliever's fright.
He who shall hurt the little wren
Shall never be belov'd by men.
He who the ox to wrath has mov'd
Shall never be by woman lov'd.
The wanton boy that kills the fly
Shall feel the spider's enmity.
He who torments the chafer's sprite
Weaves a bower in endless night.
The caterpillar on the leaf
Repeats to thee thy mother's grief.
Kill not the moth nor butterfly,
For the last judgment draweth nigh.
He who shall train the horse to war
Shall never pass the polar bar.
The beggar's dog and widow's cat,
Feed them and thou wilt grow fat.
The gnat that sings his summer's song
Poison gets from slander's tongue.
The poison of the snake and newt
Is the sweat of envy's foot.
The poison of the honey bee
Is the artist's jealousy.

The prince's robes and beggar's rags
Are toadstools on the miser's bags.
A truth that's told with bad intent
Beats all the lies you can invent.
It is right it should be so;
Man was made for joy and woe;
And when this we rightly know,
Thro' the world we safely go.
Joy and woe are woven fine,
A clothing for the soul divine.

Under every grief and pine
Runs a joy with silken twine.
The babe is more than swaddling bands;
Throughout all these human lands
Tools were made, and born were hands,
Every farmer understands.
Every tear from every eye
Becomes a babe in eternity;
This is caught by females bright,
And return'd to its own delight.
The bleat, the bark, bellow, and roar,
Are waves that beat on heaven's shore.
The babe that weeps the rod beneath
Writes revenge in realms of death.
The beggar's rags, fluttering in air,
Does to rags the heavens tear.
The soldier, arm'd with sword and gun,
Palsied strikes the summer's sun.
The poor man's farthing is worth more
Than all the gold on Afric's shore.
One mite wrung from the lab'rer's hands
Shall buy and sell the miser's lands;
Or, if protected from on high,
Does that whole nation sell and buy.
He who mocks the infant's faith
Shall be mock'd in age and death.
He who shall teach the child to doubt
The rotting grave shall ne'er get out.
He who respects the infant's faith
Triumphs over hell and death.
The child's toys and the old man's reasons
Are the fruits of the two seasons.
The questioner, who sits so sly,
Shall never know how to reply.
He who replies to words of doubt
Doth put the light of knowledge out.
The strongest poison ever known
Came from Caesar's laurel crown.

Nought can deform the human race
Like to the armour's iron brace.
When gold and gems adorn the plow,
To peaceful arts shall envy bow.
A riddle, or the cricket's cry,
Is to doubt a fit reply.
The emmet's inch and eagle's mile
Make lame philosophy to smile.
He who doubts from what he sees
Will ne'er believe, do what you please.
If the sun and moon should doubt,
They'd immediately go out.
To be in a passion you good may do,
But no good if a passion is in you.
The whore and gambler, by the state
Licensed, build that nation's fate.
The harlot's cry from street to street
Shall weave old England's winding-sheet.
The winner's shout, the loser's curse,
Dance before dead England's hearse.
Every night and every morn
Some to misery are born,
Every morn and every night
Some are born to sweet delight.
Some are born to sweet delight,
Some are born to endless night.
We are led to believe a lie
When we see not thro' the eye,
Which was born in a night to perish in a night,
When the soul slept in beams of light.
God appears, and God is light,
To those poor souls who dwell in night;
But does a human form display
To those who dwell in realms of day.

A POISON TREE

by William Blake

I was angry with my friend:
I told my wrath, my wrath did end.
I was angry with my foe:
I told it not, my wrath did grow.

And I watered it in fears,
Night and morning with my tears;
And I sunned it with smiles,
And with soft deceitful wiles.

And it grew both day and night,
Till it bore an apple bright.
And my foe beheld it shine.
And he knew that it was mine,

And into my garden stole
When the night had veiled the pole;
In the morning glad I see
My foe outstretched beneath the tree.

THE TYGER

by William Blake

Tyger Tyger, burning bright,
In the forests of the night;
What immortal hand or eye,
Could frame thy fearful symmetry?

In what distant deeps or skies.
Burnt the fire of thine eyes?
On what wings dare he aspire?
What the hand, dare seize the fire?

And what shoulder, & what art,
Could twist the sinews of thy heart?
And when thy heart began to beat,
What dread hand? & what dread feet?

What the hammer? what the chain,
In what furnace was thy brain?
What the anvil? what dread grasp,
Dare its deadly terrors clasp!

When the stars threw down their spears
And water'd heaven with their tears:
Did he smile his work to see?
Did he who made the Lamb make thee?

Tyger Tyger burning bright,
In the forests of the night:
What immortal hand or eye,
Dare frame thy fearful symmetry?

TO MY DEAR AND LOVING HUSBAND

by Anne Bradstreet

If ever two were one, then surely we.
If ever man were loved by wife, than thee;
If ever wife was happy in a man,
Compare with me, ye women, if you can.

I prize thy love more than whole mines of gold,
Or all the riches that the East doth hold.
My love is such that rivers cannot quench,
Nor aught by love from thee give recompense.

Thy love is such I can no way reply;
The heavens reward thee manifold, I pray.
Then while we live, in love let's so persever,
That when we live no more we may live ever.

THE SOLDIER

by Rupert Brooke

If I should die, think only this of me:
    That there's some corner of a foreign field
That is for ever England. There shall be
    In that rich earth a richer dust concealed;
A dust whom England bore, shaped, made aware,
    Gave, once, her flowers to love, her ways to roam,
A body of England's, breathing English air,
    Washed by the rivers, blest by suns of home.

And think, this heart, all evil shed away,
    A pulse in the eternal mind, no less
        Gives somewhere back the thoughts by England given;
Her sights and sounds; dreams happy as her day;
    And laughter, learnt of friends; and gentleness,
        In hearts at peace, under an English heaven.

SONNET 43:
HOW DO I LOVE THEE?

by Elizabeth Barrett Browning

How do I love thee? Let me count the ways.
I love thee to the depth and breadth and height
My soul can reach, when feeling out of sight
For the ends of being and ideal grace.
I love thee to the level of every day's
Most quiet need, by sun and candle-light.
I love thee freely, as men strive for right.
I love thee purely, as they turn from praise.
I love thee with the passion put to use
In my old griefs, and with my childhood's faith.
I love thee with a love I seemed to lose
With my lost saints. I love thee with the breath,
Smiles, tears, of all my life; and, if God choose,
I shall but love thee better after death.

LIFE IN A LOVE

by Robert Browning

Escape me?
Never—-
Beloved!
While I am I, and you are you,
 So long as the world contains us both,
 Me the loving and you the loth
While the one eludes, must the other pursue.
My life is a fault at last, I fear:
 It seems too much like a fate, indeed!
 Though I do my best I shall scarce succeed.
But what if I fail of my purpose here?
It is but to keep the nerves at strain,
 To dry one's eyes and laugh at a fall,
And, baffled, get up and begin again,—-
 So the Chase takes up one's life ' that's all.
While, look but once from your farthest bound
 At me so deep in the dust and dark,
No sooner the old hope goes to ground
 Than a new one, straight to the self-same mark,
I shape me—-
Ever
Removed!

MY LAST DUCHESS
by Robert Browning

FERRARA

That's my last Duchess painted on the wall,
Looking as if she were alive. I call
That piece a wonder, now; Fra Pandolf's hands
Worked busily a day, and there she stands.
Will't please you sit and look at her? I said
"Fra Pandolf" by design, for never read
Strangers like you that pictured countenance,
The depth and passion of its earnest glance,
But to myself they turned (since none puts by
The curtain I have drawn for you, but I)
And seemed as they would ask me, if they durst,
How such a glance came there; so, not the first
Are you to turn and ask thus. Sir, 'twas not
Her husband's presence only, called that spot
Of joy into the Duchess' cheek; perhaps
Fra Pandolf chanced to say, "Her mantle laps
Over my lady's wrist too much," or "Paint
Must never hope to reproduce the faint
Half-flush that dies along her throat." Such stuff
Was courtesy, she thought, and cause enough
For calling up that spot of joy. She had
A heart—how shall I say?— too soon made glad,
Too easily impressed; she liked whate'er
She looked on, and her looks went everywhere.
Sir, 'twas all one! My favour at her breast,
The dropping of the daylight in the West,

The bough of cherries some officious fool
Broke in the orchard for her, the white mule
She rode with round the terrace—all and each
Would draw from her alike the approving speech,
Or blush, at least. She thanked men—good! but thanked
Somehow—I know not how—as if she ranked
My gift of a nine-hundred-years-old name
With anybody's gift. Who'd stoop to blame
This sort of trifling? Even had you skill
In speech—which I have not—to make your will
Quite clear to such an one, and say, "Just this
Or that in you disgusts me; here you miss,
Or there exceed the mark"—and if she let
Herself be lessoned so, nor plainly set
Her wits to yours, forsooth, and made excuse—
E'en then would be some stooping; and I choose
Never to stoop. Oh, sir, she smiled, no doubt,
Whene'er I passed her; but who passed without
Much the same smile? This grew; I gave commands;
Then all smiles stopped together. There she stands
As if alive. Will't please you rise? We'll meet
The company below, then. I repeat,
The Count your master's known munificence
Is ample warrant that no just pretense
Of mine for dowry will be disallowed;
Though his fair daughter's self, as I avowed
At starting, is my object. Nay, we'll go
Together down, sir. Notice Neptune, though,
Taming a sea-horse, thought a rarity,
Which Claus of Innsbruck cast in bronze for me!

THANATOPSIS

by William Cullen Bryant

To him who in the love of nature holds
Communion with her visible forms, she speaks
A various language; for his gayer hours
She has a voice of gladness, and a smile
And eloquence of beauty, and she glides
Into his darker musings, with a mild
And healing sympathy, that steals away
Their sharpness, ere he is aware. When thoughts
Of the last bitter hour come like a blight
Over thy spirit, and sad images
Of the stern agony, and shroud, and pall,
And breathless darkness, and the narrow house,
Make thee to shudder, and grow sick at heart;—
Go forth, under the open sky, and list
To Nature's teachings, while from all around—
Earth and her waters, and the depths of air,—
Comes a still voice—Yet a few days, and thee
The all-beholding sun shall see no more
In all his course; nor yet in the cold ground,
Where thy pale form was laid, with many tears,
Nor in the embrace of ocean, shall exist
Thy image. Earth, that nourished thee,shall claim
Thy growth, to be resolved to earth again,
And, lost each human trace, surrendering up
Thine individual being, shalt thou go
To mix for ever with the elements,
To be a brother to the insensible rock

And to the sluggish clod, which the rude swain
Turns with his share, and treads upon. The oak
Shall send his roots abroad, and pierce thy mould.

  Yet not to thine eternal resting-place
Shalt thou retire alone—nor couldst thou wish
Couch more magnificent. Thou shalt lie down
With patriarchs of the infant world—with kings,
The powerful of the earth—the wise, the good,
Fair forms, and hoary seers of ages past,
All in one mighty sepulchre.—The hills
Rock-ribbed and ancient as the sun,—the vales
Sketching in pensive quietness between;
The venerable woods—rivers that move
In majesty, and the complaining brooks
That make the meadows green; and, poured round all,
Old ocean's gray and melancholy waste,—
Are but the solemn decorations all
Of the great tomb of man. The golden sun,
The planets, all the infinite host of heaven,
Are shining on the sad abodes of death,
Through the still lapse of ages. All that tread
The globe are but a handful to the tribes
That slumber in its bosom.—Take the wings
Of morning—and the Barcan desert pierce,
Or lose thyself in the continuous woods
Where rolls the Oregan, and hears no sound,
Save his own dashings—yet—the dead are there:
And millions in those solitudes, since first
The flight of years began, have laid them down
In their last sleep—the dead reign there alone.
So shalt thou rest—and what if thou withdraw
Unheeded by the living—and no friend
Take note of thy departure? All that breathe
Will share thy destiny. The gay will laugh
When thou art gone, the solemn brood of care

Plod on, and each one as before will chase
His favourite phantom; yet all these shall leave
Their mirth and their employments, and shall come,
And make their bed with thee. As the long train
Of ages glide away, the sons of men,
The youth in life's green spring, and he who goes
In the full strength of years, matron, and maid,
And the sweet babe, and the gray-headed man,—
Shall one by one be gathered to thy side,
By those, who in their turn shall follow them.

　　So live, that when thy summons comes to join
The innumerable caravan, that moves
To that mysterious realm, where each shall take
His chamber in the silent halls of death,
Thou go not, like the quarry-slave at night,
Scourged to his dungeon, but, sustained and soothed
By an unfaltering trust, approach thy grave,
Like one who wraps the drapery of his couch
About him, and lies down to pleasant dreams.

A RED, RED ROSE

by Robert Burns

O my Luve is like a red, red rose
    That's newly sprung in June;
O my Luve is like the melody
    That's sweetly played in tune.

So fair art thou, my bonnie lass,
    So deep in luve am I;
And I will luve thee still, my dear,
    Till a' the seas gang dry.

Till a' the seas gang dry, my dear,
    And the rocks melt wi' the sun;
I will love thee still, my dear,
    While the sands o' life shall run.

And fare thee weel, my only luve!
    And fare thee weel awhile!
And I will come again, my luve,
    Though it were ten thousand mile.

AULD LANG SYNE

by Robert Burns

Should auld acquaintance be forgot,
And never brought to mind?
Should auld acquaintance be forgot,
And auld lang syne!
     Chorus:
For auld lang syne, my dear,
     For auld lang syne.
      We'll tak a cup o' kindness yet,
     For auld lang syne.
And surely ye'll be your pint stowp!
And surely I'll be mine!
And we'll tak a cup o' kindness yet,
For auld lang syne.
    Chorus
We twa hae run about the braes,
And pou'd the gowans fine;
But we've wander'd mony a weary fit,
Sin' auld lang syne.
    Chorus
We twa hae paidl'd in the burn,
Frae morning sun till dine;
But seas between us braid hae roar'd
Sin' auld lang syne.
    Chorus
And there's a hand, my trusty fere!
And gie's a hand o' thine!
And we'll tak a right gude-willie waught,
For auld lang syne.
    Chorus

TO A MOUSE

by Robert Burns

On Turning up her Nest with the Plow, November, 1785
Wee, sleeket, cowran, tim'rous beastie,
O, what a panic's in thy breastie!
Thou need na start awa sae hasty,
      Wi' bickerin brattle!
I wad be laith to rin an' chase thee
      Wi' murd'ring pattle!

I'm truly sorry Man's dominion
Has broken Nature's social union,
An' justifies that ill opinion,
      Which makes thee startle,
At me, thy poor, earth-born companion,
      An' fellow-mortal!

I doubt na, whyles, but thou may thieve;
What then? poor beastie, thou maun live!
A daimen-icker in a thrave
      'S a sma' request:
I'll get a blessin wi' the lave,
      An' never miss 't!

Thy wee-bit housie, too, in ruin!
It's silly wa's the win's are strewin!
An' naething, now, to big a new ane,

O' foggage green!
An' bleak December's winds ensuin,
Baith snell an' keen!

Thou saw the fields laid bare an' waste,
An' weary Winter comin fast,
An' cozie here, beneath the blast,
Thou thought to dwell,
Till crash! the cruel coulter past
Out thro' thy cell.

That wee-bit heap o' leaves an' stibble
Has cost thee monie a weary nibble!
Now thou's turn'd out, for a' thy trouble,
But house or hald,
To thole the Winter's sleety dribble,
An' cranreuch cauld!

... But Mousie, thou art no thy-lane,
In proving foresight may be vain:
The best laid schemes o' Mice an' Men
Gang aft agley,
An' lea'e us nought but grief an' pain,
For promis'd joy!

Still, thou art blest, compar'd wi' me!
The present only toucheth thee:
But Och! I backward cast my e'e,
On prospects drear!
An' forward tho' I canna see,
I guess an' fear!

SHE WALKS IN BEAUTY

by George Gordon, Lord Byron

She walks in beauty, like the night
    Of cloudless climes and starry skies;
And all that's best of dark and bright
    Meet in her aspect and her eyes;
Thus mellowed to that tender light
    Which heaven to gaudy day denies.
One shade the more, one ray the less,
    Had half impaired the nameless grace
Which waves in every raven tress,
    Or softly lightens o'er her face;
Where thoughts serenely sweet express,
    How pure, how dear their dwelling-place.
And on that cheek, and o'er that brow,
    So soft, so calm, yet eloquent,
The smiles that win, the tints that glow,
    But tell of days in goodness spent,
A mind at peace with all below,
    A heart whose love is innocent!

THERE IS PLEASURE IN THE PATHLESS WOODS

by George Gordon, Lord Byron

There is a pleasure in the pathless woods,
There is a rapture on the lonely shore,
There is society, where none intrudes,
By the deep sea, and music in its roar:
I love not man the less, but Nature more,
From these our interviews, in which I steal
From all I may be, or have been before,
To mingle with the Universe, and feel
What I can ne'er express, yet cannot all conceal.

WHEN WE TWO PARTED

by George Gordon, Lord Byron

When we two parted
When we two parted
   In silence and tears,
Half broken-hearted
   To sever for years,
Pale grew thy cheek and cold,
   Colder thy kiss;
Truly that hour foretold
   Sorrow to this.

The dew of the morning
   Sunk chill on my brow—
It felt like the warning
   Of what I feel now.
Thy vows are all broken,
   And light is thy fame;
I hear thy name spoken,
   And share in its shame.

They name thee before me,
   A knell to mine ear;
A shudder comes o'er me—
   Why wert thou so dear?

They know not I knew thee,
  Who knew thee too well—
Long, long shall I rue thee,
  Too deeply to tell.

In secret we met—
  In silence I grieve,
That thy heart could forget,
  Thy spirit deceive.
If I should meet thee
  After long years,
How should I greet thee?—
  With silence and tears.

JABBERWOCKY
by Lewis Carroll

'Twas brillig, and the slithy toves
　Did gyre and gimble in the wabe;
All mimsy were the borogoves,
　And the mome raths outgrabe.
"Beware the Jabberwock, my son
　The jaws that bite, the claws that catch!
Beware the Jubjub bird, and shun
　The frumious Bandersnatch!"
He took his vorpal sword in hand;
　Long time the manxome foe he sought—
So rested he by the Tumtum tree,
　And stood awhile in thought.
And, as in uffish thought he stood,
　The Jabberwock, with eyes of flame,
Came whiffling through the tulgey wood,
　And burbled as it came!
One, two! One, two! And through and through
　The vorpal blade went snicker-snack!
He left it dead, and with its head
　He went galumphing back.
"And hast thou slain the Jabberwock?
　Come to my arms, my beamish boy!
O frabjous day! Callooh! Callay!"
　He chortled in his joy.
'Twas brillig, and the slithy toves
　Did gyre and gimble in the wabe;
All mimsy were the borogoves,
　And the mome raths outgrabe.

FROST AT MIDNIGHT

by Samuel Taylor Coleridge

The frost performs its secret ministry,
Unhelped by any wind. The owlet's cry
Came loud—and hark, again! loud as before.
The inmates of my cottage, all at rest,
Have left me to that solitude, which suits
Abstruser musings: save that at my side
My cradled infant slumbers peacefully.
'Tis calm indeed! so calm, that it disturbs
And vexes meditation with its strange
And extreme silentness. Sea, hill, and wood,
This populous village! Sea, and hill, and wood,
With all the numberless goings-on of life,
Inaudible as dreams! the thin blue flame
Lies on my low-burnt fire, and quivers not;
Only that film, which fluttered on the grate,
Still flutters there, the sole unquiet thing.
Methinks, its motion in this hush of nature
Gives it dim sympathies with me who live,
Making it a companionable form,
Whose puny flaps and freaks the idling Spirit
By its own moods interprets, everywhere
Echo or mirror seeking of itself,
And makes a toy of Thought.

But O! how oft,
How oft, at school, with most believing mind,
Presageful, have I gazed upon the bars,
To watch that fluttering stranger! and as oft
With unclosed lids, already had I dreamt
Of my sweet birthplace, and the old church-tower,
Whose bells, the poor man's only music, rang
From morn to evening, all the hot Fair-day,
So sweetly, that they stirred and haunted me
With a wild pleasure, falling on mine ear
Most like articulate sounds of things to come!
So gazed I, till the soothing things I dreamt
Lulled me to sleep, and sleep prolonged my dreams!
And so I brooded all the following morn,
Awed by the stern preceptor's face, mine eye
Fixed with mock study on my swimming book:
Save if the door half opened, and I snatched
A hasty glance, and still my heart leaped up,
For still I hoped to see the stranger's face,
Townsman, or aunt, or sister more beloved,
My playmate when we both were clothed alike!

Dear babe, that sleepest cradled by my side,
Whose gentle breathings, heard in this deep calm,
Fill up the interspersed vacancies
And momentary pauses of the thought!
My babe so beautiful! it thrills my heart
With tender gladness, thus to look at thee,
And think that thou shalt learn far other lore
And in far other scenes! For I was reared
In the great city, pent 'mid cloisters dim,
And saw nought lovely but the sky and stars.
But thou, my babe! shalt wander like a breeze
By lakes and sandy shores, beneath the crags
Of ancient mountain, and beneath the clouds,
Which image in their bulk both lakes and shores

And mountain crags: so shalt thou see and hear
The lovely shapes and sounds intelligible
Of that eternal language, which thy God
Utters, who fro eternity doth teach
Himself in all, and all things in himself.
Great universal Teacher! he shall mould
They spirit, and by giving make it ask.

    Therefore all seasons shall be sweet to thee,
Whether the summer clothe the general earth
With greenness, or the redbreast sit and sing
Betwixt the tufts of snow on the bare branch
Of mossy apple-tree, while the nigh thatch
Smokes in the sunthaw; whether the eve-drops fall
Heard only in the trances of the blast,
Or if the secret ministry of frost
Shall hang them up in silent icicles,
Quietly shining to the quiet Moon.

KUBLA KHAN

by Samuel Taylor Coleridge

Or, a Vision in a Dream. A Fragment.

In Xanadu did Kubla Khan
A stately pleasure-dome decree:
Where Alph, the sacred river, ran
Through caverns measureless to man
    Down to a sunless sea.
So twice five miles of fertile ground
With walls and towers were girdled round;
And there were gardens bright with sinuous rills,
Where blossomed many an incense-bearing tree;
And here were forests ancient as the hills,
Enfolding sunny spots of greenery.

But oh! that deep romantic chasm which slanted
Down the green hill athwart a cedarn cover!
A savage place! as holy and enchanted
As e'er beneath a waning moon was haunted
By woman wailing for her demon-lover!
And from this chasm, with ceaseless turmoil seething,
As if this earth in fast thick pants were breathing,
A mighty fountain momently was forced:
Amid whose swift half-intermitted burst
Huge fragments vaulted like rebounding hail,
Or chaffy grain beneath the thresher's flail:

And mid these dancing rocks at once and ever
It flung up momently the sacred river.
Five miles meandering with a mazy motion
Through wood and dale the sacred river ran,
Then reached the caverns measureless to man,
And sank in tumult to a lifeless ocean;
And 'mid this tumult Kubla heard from far
Ancestral voices prophesying war!
    The shadow of the dome of pleasure
     Floated midway on the waves;
     Where was heard the mingled measure
     From the fountain and the caves.
It was a miracle of rare device,
A sunny pleasure-dome with caves of ice!
    A damsel with a dulcimer
    In a vision once I saw:
    It was an Abyssinian maid
    And on her dulcimer she played,
    Singing of Mount Abora.
    Could I revive within me
    Her symphony and song,
    To such a deep delight 'twould win me,
That with music loud and long,
I would build that dome in air,
That sunny dome! those caves of ice!
And all who heard should see them there,
And all should cry, Beware! Beware!
His flashing eyes, his floating hair!
Weave a circle round him thrice,
And close your eyes with holy dread
For he on honey-dew hath fed,
And drunk the milk of Paradise.

THE RIME OF THE ANCIENT MARINER

by Samuel Taylor Coleridge

Part I.

It is an ancient Mariner,
And he stoppeth one of three.
"By thy long grey beard and glittering eye,
Now wherefore stopp'st thou me?

"The Bridegroom's doors are opened wide,
And I am next of kin;
The guests are met, the feast is set:
May'st hear the merry din."

He holds him with his skinny hand,
"There was a ship," quoth he.
"Hold off! unhand me, grey-beard loon!"
Eftsoons his hand dropt he.

He holds him with his glittering eye—
The Wedding-Guest stood still,
And listens like a three years child:
The Mariner hath his will.

The Wedding-Guest sat on a stone:
He cannot chuse but hear;
And thus spake on that ancient man,
The bright-eyed Mariner.

The ship was cheered, the harbour cleared,
Merrily did we drop
Below the kirk, below the hill,
Below the light-house top.

The Sun came up upon the left,
Out of the sea came he!
And he shone bright, and on the right
Went down into the sea.

Higher and higher every day,
Till over the mast at noon—
The Wedding-Guest here beat his breast,
For he heard the loud bassoon.

The bride hath paced into the hall,
Red as a rose is she;
Nodding their heads before her goes
The merry minstrelsy.

The Wedding-Guest he beat his breast,
Yet he cannot chuse but hear;
And thus spake on that ancient man,
The bright-eyed Mariner.

And now the STORM-BLAST came, and he
Was tyrannous and strong:
He struck with his o'ertaking wings,
And chased south along.

With sloping masts and dipping prow,
As who pursued with yell and blow
Still treads the shadow of his foe
And forward bends his head,
The ship drove fast, loud roared the blast,
And southward aye we fled.

And now there came both mist and snow,
And it grew wondrous cold:
And ice, mast-high, came floating by,
As green as emerald.

And through the drifts the snowy clifts
Did send a dismal sheen:
Nor shapes of men nor beasts we ken—
The ice was all between.

The ice was here, the ice was there,
The ice was all around:
It cracked and growled, and roared and howled,
Like noises in a swound!

At length did cross an Albatross:
Thorough the fog it came;
As if it had been a Christian soul,
We hailed it in God's name.

It ate the food it ne'er had eat,
And round and round it flew.
The ice did split with a thunder-fit;
The helmsman steered us through!

And a good south wind sprung up behind;
The Albatross did follow,
And every day, for food or play,
Came to the mariners' hollo!

In mist or cloud, on mast or shroud,
It perched for vespers nine;
Whiles all the night, through fog-smoke white,
Glimmered the white Moon-shine.

"God save thee, ancient Mariner!
From the fiends, that plague thee thus!—
Why look'st thou so?"—With my cross-bow
I shot the ALBATROSS.

Part II.

The Sun now rose upon the right:
Out of the sea came he,
Still hid in mist, and on the left
Went down into the sea.

And the good south wind still blew behind
But no sweet bird did follow,
Nor any day for food or play
Came to the mariners' hollo!

And I had done an hellish thing,
And it would work 'em woe:
For all averred, I had killed the bird
That made the breeze to blow.
Ah wretch! said they, the bird to slay
That made the breeze to blow!

Nor dim nor red, like God's own head,
The glorious Sun uprist:
Then all averred, I had killed the bird
That brought the fog and mist.
'Twas right, said they, such birds to slay,
That bring the fog and mist.

The fair breeze blew, the white foam flew,
The furrow followed free:
We were the first that ever burst
Into that silent sea.

Down dropt the breeze, the sails dropt down,
'Twas sad as sad could be;
And we did speak only to break
The silence of the sea!

All in a hot and copper sky,
The bloody Sun, at noon,
Right up above the mast did stand,
No bigger than the Moon.

Day after day, day after day,
We stuck, nor breath nor motion;
As idle as a painted ship
Upon a painted ocean.

Water, water, every where,
And all the boards did shrink;
Water, water, every where,
Nor any drop to drink.

The very deep did rot: O Christ!
That ever this should be!
Yea, slimy things did crawl with legs
Upon the slimy sea.

About, about, in reel and rout
The death-fires danced at night;
The water, like a witch's oils,
Burnt green, and blue and white.

And some in dreams assured were
Of the spirit that plagued us so:
Nine fathom deep he had followed us
From the land of mist and snow.

And every tongue, through utter drought,
Was withered at the root;
We could not speak, no more than if
We had been choked with soot.
Ah! well a-day! what evil looks

Had I from old and young!
Instead of the cross, the Albatross
About my neck was hung.

Part III.

There passed a weary time. Each throat
Was parched, and glazed each eye.
A weary time! a weary time!
How glazed each weary eye,
When looking westward, I beheld
A something in the sky.

At first it seemed a little speck,
And then it seemed a mist:
It moved and moved, and took at last
A certain shape, I wist.

A speck, a mist, a shape, I wist!
And still it neared and neared:
As if it dodged a water-sprite,
It plunged and tacked and veered.

With throats unslaked, with black lips baked,
We could not laugh nor wail;
Through utter drought all dumb we stood!
I bit my arm, I sucked the blood,
And cried, A sail! a sail!

With throats unslaked, with black lips baked,
Agape they heard me call:
Gramercy! they for joy did grin,
And all at once their breath drew in,
As they were drinking all.

See! see! (I cried) she tacks no more!
Hither to work us weal;
Without a breeze, without a tide,
She steadies with upright keel!

The western wave was all a-flame
The day was well nigh done!
Almost upon the western wave
Rested the broad bright Sun;
When that strange shape drove suddenly
Betwixt us and the Sun.

And straight the Sun was flecked with bars,
(Heaven's Mother send us grace!)
As if through a dungeon-grate he peered,
With broad and burning face.

Alas! (thought I, and my heart beat loud)
How fast she nears and nears!
Are those her sails that glance in the Sun,
Like restless gossameres!

Are those her ribs through which the Sun
Did peer, as through a grate?
And is that Woman all her crew?
Is that a DEATH? and are there two?
Is DEATH that woman's mate?
Her lips were red, her looks were free,

Her locks were yellow as gold:
Her skin was as white as leprosy,
The Night-Mare LIFE-IN-DEATH was she,
Who thicks man's blood with cold.

The naked hulk alongside came,
And the twain were casting dice;
"The game is done! I've won! I've won!"
Quoth she, and whistles thrice.

The Sun's rim dips; the stars rush out:
At one stride comes the dark;
With far-heard whisper, o'er the sea.
Off shot the spectre-bark.

We listened and looked sideways up!
Fear at my heart, as at a cup,
My life-blood seemed to sip!

The stars were dim, and thick the night,
The steersman's face by his lamp gleamed white;
From the sails the dew did drip—
Till clombe above the eastern bar
The horned Moon, with one bright star
Within the nether tip.

One after one, by the star-dogged Moon
Too quick for groan or sigh,
Each turned his face with a ghastly pang,
And cursed me with his eye.

Four times fifty living men,
(And I heard nor sigh nor groan)
With heavy thump, a lifeless lump,
They dropped down one by one.

The souls did from their bodies fly,—
They fled to bliss or woe!
And every soul, it passed me by,
Like the whizz of my CROSS-BOW!

Part IV.

"I fear thee, ancient Mariner!
I fear thy skinny hand!
And thou art long, and lank, and brown,
As is the ribbed sea-sand.
"I fear thee and thy glittering eye,
And thy skinny hand, so brown."—
Fear not, fear not, thou Wedding-Guest!
This body dropt not down.

Alone, alone, all, all alone,
Alone on a wide wide sea!
And never a saint took pity on
My soul in agony.

The many men, so beautiful!
And they all dead did lie:
And a thousand thousand slimy things
Lived on; and so did I.

I looked upon the rotting sea,
And drew my eyes away;
I looked upon the rotting deck,
And there the dead men lay.

I looked to Heaven, and tried to pray:
But or ever a prayer had gusht,
A wicked whisper came, and made
my heart as dry as dust.

I closed my lids, and kept them close,
And the balls like pulses beat;
For the sky and the sea, and the sea and the sky
Lay like a load on my weary eye,
And the dead were at my feet.

The cold sweat melted from their limbs,
Nor rot nor reek did they:
The look with which they looked on me
Had never passed away.

An orphan's curse would drag to Hell
A spirit from on high;
But oh! more horrible than that
Is a curse in a dead man's eye!
Seven days, seven nights, I saw that curse,
And yet I could not die.

The moving Moon went up the sky,
And no where did abide:
Softly she was going up,
And a star or two beside.

Her beams bemocked the sultry main,
Like April hoar-frost spread;
But where the ship's huge shadow lay,
The charmed water burnt alway
A still and awful red.

Beyond the shadow of the ship,
I watched the water-snakes:
They moved in tracks of shining white,
And when they reared, the elfish light
Fell off in hoary flakes.

Within the shadow of the ship
I watched their rich attire:
Blue, glossy green, and velvet black,
They coiled and swam; and every track
Was a flash of golden fire.

O happy living things! no tongue
Their beauty might declare:
A spring of love gushed from my heart,
And I blessed them unaware:
Sure my kind saint took pity on me,
And I blessed them unaware.

The self same moment I could pray;
And from my neck so free
The Albatross fell off, and sank
Like lead into the sea.

Part V.

Oh sleep! it is a gentle thing,
Beloved from pole to pole!
To Mary Queen the praise be given!
She sent the gentle sleep from Heaven,
That slid into my soul.

The silly buckets on the deck,
That had so long remained,
I dreamt that they were filled with dew;
And when I awoke, it rained.

My lips were wet, my throat was cold,
My garments all were dank;
Sure I had drunken in my dreams,
And still my body drank.

I moved, and could not feel my limbs:
I was so light—almost
I thought that I had died in sleep,
And was a blessed ghost.

And soon I heard a roaring wind:
It did not come anear;
But with its sound it shook the sails,
That were so thin and sere.

The upper air burst into life!
And a hundred fire-flags sheen,
To and fro they were hurried about!
And to and fro, and in and out,
The wan stars danced between.

And the coming wind did roar more loud,
And the sails did sigh like sedge;
And the rain poured down from one black cloud;
The Moon was at its edge.

The thick black cloud was cleft, and still
The Moon was at its side:
Like waters shot from some high crag,
The lightning fell with never a jag,
A river steep and wide.

The loud wind never reached the ship,
Yet now the ship moved on!
Beneath the lightning and the Moon
The dead men gave a groan.

They groaned, they stirred, they all uprose,
Nor spake, nor moved their eyes;
It had been strange, even in a dream,
To have seen those dead men rise.

The helmsman steered, the ship moved on;
Yet never a breeze up blew;
The mariners all 'gan work the ropes,
Where they were wont to do:
They raised their limbs like lifeless tools—
We were a ghastly crew.

The body of my brother's son,
Stood by me, knee to knee:
The body and I pulled at one rope,
But he said nought to me.
"I fear thee, ancient Mariner!"
Be calm, thou Wedding-Guest!
'Twas not those souls that fled in pain,
Which to their corses came again,
But a troop of spirits blest:

For when it dawned—they dropped their arms,
And clustered round the mast;
Sweet sounds rose slowly through their mouths,
And from their bodies passed.

Around, around, flew each sweet sound,
Then darted to the Sun;
Slowly the sounds came back again,
Now mixed, now one by one.

Sometimes a-dropping from the sky
I heard the sky-lark sing;
Sometimes all little birds that are,
How they seemed to fill the sea and air
With their sweet jargoning!

And now 'twas like all instruments,
Now like a lonely flute;
And now it is an angel's song,
That makes the Heavens be mute.

It ceased; yet still the sails made on
A pleasant noise till noon,
A noise like of a hidden brook
In the leafy month of June,
That to the sleeping woods all night
Singeth a quiet tune.

Till noon we quietly sailed on,
Yet never a breeze did breathe:
Slowly and smoothly went the ship,
Moved onward from beneath.

Under the keel nine fathom deep,
From the land of mist and snow,
The spirit slid: and it was he
That made the ship to go.
The sails at noon left off their tune,
And the ship stood still also.

The Sun, right up above the mast,
Had fixed her to the ocean:
But in a minute she 'gan stir,
With a short uneasy motion—
Backwards and forwards half her length
With a short uneasy motion.

Then like a pawing horse let go,
She made a sudden bound:
It flung the blood into my head,
And I fell down in a swound.

How long in that same fit I lay,
I have not to declare;
But ere my living life returned,
I heard and in my soul discerned
Two VOICES in the air.

"Is it he?" quoth one, "Is this the man?
By him who died on cross,
With his cruel bow he laid full low,
The harmless Albatross.

"The spirit who bideth by himself
In the land of mist and snow,
He loved the bird that loved the man
Who shot him with his bow."

The other was a softer voice,
As soft as honey-dew:
Quoth he, "The man hath penance done,
And penance more will do."

Part VI.

First Voice.
But tell me, tell me! speak again,
Thy soft response renewing—
What makes that ship drive on so fast?
What is the OCEAN doing?

Second Voice.
Still as a slave before his lord,
The OCEAN hath no blast; His great bright
eye most silently
Up to the Moon is cast—

If he may know which way to go;
For she guides him smooth or grim
See, brother, see! how graciously
She looketh down on him.

      First Voice.
But why drives on that ship so fast,
Without or wave or wind?

      Second Voice.
The air is cut away before,
And closes from behind.

Fly, brother, fly! more high, more high
Or we shall be belated:
For slow and slow that ship will go,
When the Mariner's trance is abated.

I woke, and we were sailing on
As in a gentle weather:
'Twas night, calm night, the Moon was high;
The dead men stood together.

All stood together on the deck,
For a charnel-dungeon fitter:
All fixed on me their stony eyes,
That in the Moon did glitter.

The pang, the curse, with which they died,
Had never passed away:
I could not draw my eyes from theirs,
Nor turn them up to pray.

And now this spell was snapt: once more
I viewed the ocean green.
And looked far forth, yet little saw
Of what had else been seen—

Like one that on a lonesome road
Doth walk in fear and dread,
And having once turned round walks on,
And turns no more his head;
Because he knows, a frightful fiend
Doth close behind him tread.

But soon there breathed a wind on me,
Nor sound nor motion made:
Its path was not upon the sea,
In ripple or in shade.
It raised my hair, it fanned my cheek
Like a meadow-gale of spring—
It mingled strangely with my fears,
Yet it felt like a welcoming.

Swiftly, swiftly flew the ship,
Yet she sailed softly too:
Sweetly, sweetly blew the breeze—
On me alone it blew.

Oh! dream of joy! is this indeed
The light-house top I see?
Is this the hill? is this the kirk?
Is this mine own countree!

We drifted o'er the harbour-bar,
And I with sobs did pray—
O let me be awake, my God!
Or let me sleep alway.

The harbour-bay was clear as glass,
So smoothly it was strewn!
And on the bay the moonlight lay,
And the shadow of the moon.

The rock shone bright, the kirk no less,
That stands above the rock:
The moonlight steeped in silentness
The steady weathercock.

And the bay was white with silent light,
Till rising from the same,
Full many shapes, that shadows were,
In crimson colours came.

A little distance from the prow
Those crimson shadows were:
I turned my eyes upon the deck—
Oh, Christ! what saw I there!

Each corse lay flat, lifeless and flat,
And, by the holy rood!
A man all light, a seraph-man,
On every corse there stood.

This seraph band, each waved his hand:
It was a heavenly sight
They stood as signals to the land,
Each one a lovely light:

This seraph-band, each waved his hand,
No voice did they impart—
No voice; but oh! the silence sank
Like music on my heart.

But soon I heard the dash of oars;
I heard the Pilot's cheer;
My head was turned perforce away,
And I saw a boat appear.

The Pilot, and the Pilot's boy,
I heard them coming fast:
Dear Lord in Heaven! it was a joy
The dead men could not blast.

I saw a third—I heard his voice:
It is the Hermit good!
He singeth loud his godly hymns
That he makes in the wood.
He'll shrieve my soul, he'll wash away
The Albatross's blood.

Part VII.

This Hermit good lives in that wood
Which slopes down to the sea.
How loudly his sweet voice he rears!
He loves to talk with marineres
That come from a far countree.

He kneels at morn and noon and eve—
He hath a cushion plump:
It is the moss that wholly hides
The rotted old oak-stump.

The skiff-boat neared: I heard them talk,
"Why this is strange, I trow!
Where are those lights so many and fair,
That signal made but now?"

"Strange, by my faith!" the Hermit said—
"And they answered not our cheer!
The planks looked warped! and see those sails,
How thin they are and sere!
I never saw aught like to them,
Unless perchance it were
"Brown skeletons of leaves that lag
My forest-brook along;
When the ivy-tod is heavy with snow,
And the owlet whoops to the wolf below,
That eats the she-wolf's young."

"Dear Lord! it hath a fiendish look—
(The Pilot made reply)
I am a-feared"—"Push on, push on!"
Said the Hermit cheerily.

The boat came closer to the ship,
But I nor spake nor stirred;
The boat came close beneath the ship,
And straight a sound was heard.

Under the water it rumbled on,
Still louder and more dread:
It reached the ship, it split the bay;
The ship went down like lead.

Stunned by that loud and dreadful sound,
Which sky and ocean smote,
Like one that hath been seven days drowned
My body lay afloat;
But swift as dreams, myself I found
Within the Pilot's boat.

Upon the whirl, where sank the ship,
The boat spun round and round;
And all was still, save that the hill
Was telling of the sound.

I moved my lips—the Pilot shrieked
And fell down in a fit;
The holy Hermit raised his eyes,
And prayed where he did sit.

I took the oars: the Pilot's boy,
Who now doth crazy go,
Laughed loud and long, and all the while
His eyes went to and fro.
"Ha! ha!" quoth he, "full plain I see,
The Devil knows how to row."

And now, all in my own countree,
I stood on the firm land!
The Hermit stepped forth from the boat,
And scarcely he could stand.

"O shrieve me, shrieve me, holy man!"
The Hermit crossed his brow.
"Say quick," quoth he, "I bid thee say—
What manner of man art thou?"

Forthwith this frame of mine was
wrenched
With a woeful agony,
Which forced me to begin my tale;
And then it left me free.

Since then, at an uncertain hour,
That agony returns;
And till my ghastly tale is told,
This heart within me burns.

I pass, like night, from land to land;
I have strange power of speech;
That moment that his face I see,
I know the man that must hear me:
To him my tale I teach.

What loud uproar bursts from that door!
The wedding-guests are there:
But in the garden-bower the bride
And bride-maids singing are:
And hark the little vesper bell,
Which biddeth me to prayer!

O Wedding-Guest! this soul hath been
Alone on a wide wide sea:
So lonely 'twas, that God himself
Scarce seemed there to be.

O sweeter than the marriage-feast,
'Tis sweeter far to me,
To walk together to the kirk
With a goodly company!—

To walk together to the kirk,
And all together pray,
While each to his great Father bends,
Old men, and babes, and loving friends,
And youths and maidens gay!

Farewell, farewell! but this I tell
To thee, thou Wedding-Guest!
He prayeth well, who loveth well
Both man and bird and beast.

He prayeth best, who loveth best
All things both great and small;
For the dear God who loveth us
He made and loveth all.

The Mariner, whose eye is bright,
Whose beard with age is hoar,
Is gone: and now the Wedding-Guest
Turned from the bridegroom's door.

He went like one that hath been stunned,
And is of sense forlorn:
A sadder and a wiser man,
He rose the morrow morn.

I CARRY YOUR HEART WITH ME

by E.E. Cummings

i carry your heart with me (i carry it in
my heart) i am never without it (anywhere
i go you go, my dear; and whatever is done
by only me is your doing, my darling)
                    i fear
no fate (for you are my fate, my sweet) i want
no world (for beautiful you are my world, my true)
and it's you are whatever a moon has always meant
and whatever a sun will always sing is you

here is the deepest secret nobody knows
(here is the root of the root and the bud of the bud
and the sky of the sky of a tree called life; which grows
higher than soul can hope or mind can hide)
and this is the wonder that's keeping the stars apart

i carry your heart (i carry it in my heart)

THE LISTENERS

by Walter de la Mare

'Is there anybody there?' said the Traveller,
Knocking on the moonlit door;
And his horse in the silence champed the grasses
Of the forest's ferny floor:
And a bird flew up out of the turret,
Above the Traveller's head:
And he smote upon the door again a second time;
'Is there anybody there?' he said.
But no one descended to the Traveller;
No head from the leaf-fringed sill
Leaned over and looked into his grey eyes,
Where he stood perplexed and still.
But only a host of phantom listeners
That dwelt in the lone house then
Stood listening in the quiet of the moonlight
To that voice from the world of men:
Stood thronging the faint moonbeams on the dark stair,
That goes down to the empty hall,
Hearkening in an air stirred and shaken
By the lonely Traveller's call.
And he felt in his heart their strangeness,
Their stillness answering his cry,
While his horse moved, cropping the dark turf,
'Neath the starred and leafy sky;
For he suddenly smote on the door, even

Louder, and lifted his head:—
'Tell them I came, and no one answered,
That I kept my word,' he said.
Never the least stir made the listeners,
Though every word he spake
Fell echoing through the shadowiness of the still house
From the one man left awake:
Ay, they heard his foot upon the stirrup,
And the sound of iron on stone,
And how the silence surged softly backward,
When the plunging hoofs were gone.

BECAUSE I COULD NOT STOP FOR DEATH

by Emily Dickinson

Because I could not stop for Death –
He kindly stopped for me –
The Carriage held but just Ourselves –
And Immortality.

We slowly drove – He knew no haste
And I had put away
My labor and my leisure too,
For His Civility –

We passed the School, where Children strove
At Recess – in the Ring –
We passed the Fields of Gazing Grain –
We passed the Setting Sun –

Or rather – He passed us –
The Dews drew quivering and chill –
For only Gossamer, my Gown –
My Tippet – only Tulle –

We paused before a House that seemed
A Swelling of the Ground –
The Roof was scarcely visible –
The Cornice – in the Ground –

Since then – 'tis Centuries – and yet
Feels shorter than the Day
I first surmised the Horses' Heads
Were toward Eternity –

HOPE IS THE THING WITH FEATHERS

by Emily Dickinson

Hope is the thing with feathers
That perches in the soul,
And sings the tune without the words,
And never stops at all,

And sweetest in the gale is heard;
And sore must be the storm
That could abash the little bird
That kept so many warm.

I've heard it in the chillest land,
And on the strangest sea;
Yet, never, in extremity,
It asked a crumb of me.

I HEARD A FLY BUZZ WHEN I DIED

by Emily Dickinson

I heard a Fly buzz - when I died -
The Stillness in the Room
Was like the Stillness in the Air -
Between the Heaves of Storm -

The Eyes around - had wrung them dry -
And Breaths were gathering firm
For that last Onset - when the King
Be witnessed - in the Room -

I willed my Keepsakes - Signed away
What portion of me be
Assignable - and then it was
There interposed a Fly -

With Blue - uncertain - stumbling Buzz -
Between the light - and me -
And then the Windows failed - and then
I could not see to see -

I FELT A FUNERAL IN MY BRAIN

by Emily Dickinson

I felt a funeral in my brain,
   And mourners, to and fro,
Kept treading, treading, till it seemed
   That sense was breaking through.
And when they all were seated,
   A service like a drum
Kept beating, beating, till I thought
   My mind was going numb.
And then I heard them lift a box,
   And creak across my soul
With those same boots of lead, again.
    Then space began to toll
As all the heavens were a bell,
   And Being but an ear,
And I and silence some strange race,
   Wrecked, solitary, here.

I'M NOBODY! WHO ARE YOU?

by Emily Dickinson

I'm nobody! Who are you?
Are you nobody, too?
Then there 's a pair of us — don't tell!
They 'd banish us, you know.

How dreary to be somebody!
How public, like a frog
To tell your name the livelong day
To an admiring bog!

I TASTE A LIQUOR NEVER BREWED

by Emily Dickinson

I taste a liquor never brewed,
From tankards scooped in pearl;
Not all the vats upon the Rhine
Yield such an alcohol!

Inebriate of air am I,
And debauchee of dew,
Reeling, through endless summer days,
From inns of molten blue.

When landlords turn the drunken bee
Out of the foxglove's door,
When butterflies renounce their drams,
I shall but drink the more!

Till seraphs swing their snowy hats,
And saints to windows run,
To see the little tippler
Leaning against the sun!

IF I CAN STOP ONE HEART FROM BREAKING

by Emily Dickinson

If I can stop one heart from breaking,
I shall not live in vain;
If I can ease one life the aching,
Or cool one pain,
Or help one fainting robin
Unto his nest again,
I shall not live in vain.

MUCH MADNESS IS DIVINEST SENSE

by Emily Dickinson

Much Madness is divinest Sense -
To a discerning Eye -
Much Sense - the starkest Madness -
'Tis the Majority
In this, as all, prevail -
Assent - and you are sane -
Demur - you're straightway dangerous -
And handled with a Chain -

MY LIFE HAD STOOD – A LOADED GUN

by Emily Dickinson

My Life had stood - a Loaded Gun -
In Corners - till a Day
The Owner passed - identified -
And carried Me away -

And now We roam in Sovreign Woods -
And now We hunt the Doe -
And every time I speak for Him
The Mountains straight reply -

And do I smile, such cordial light
Opon the Valley glow -
It is as a Vesuvian face
Had let it's pleasure through -

And when at Night - Our good Day done -
I guard My Master's Head -
'Tis better than the Eider Duck's
Deep Pillow - to have shared -

To foe of His - I'm deadly foe -
None stir the second time -
On whom I lay a Yellow Eye -
Or an emphatic Thumb -

Though I than He - may longer live
He longer must - than I -
For I have but the power to kill,
Without - the power to die -

SUCCESS IS COUNTED SWEETEST

by Emily Dickinson

Success is counted sweetest
By those who ne'er succeed.
To comprehend a nectar
Requires sorest need.
Not one of all the purple host
Who took the flag to-day
Can tell the definition,
So clear, of victory,
As he, defeated, dying,
On whose forbidden ear
The distant strains of triumph
Break, agonized and clear!

TELL ALL THE TRUTH BUT TELL IT SLANT

by Emily Dickinson

Tell all the truth but tell it slant —
Success in Circuit lies
Too bright for our infirm Delight
The Truth's superb surprise
As Lightning to the Children eased
With explanation kind
The Truth must dazzle gradually
Or every man be blind —

WILD NIGHTS – WILD NIGHTS!

by Emily Dickinson

Wild nights! Wild nights!
Were I with thee,
Wild nights should be
Our luxury!

Futile the winds
To a heart in port, —
Done with the compass,
Done with the chart.

Rowing in Eden!
Ah! the sea!
Might I but moor
To-night in thee!

HOLY SONNET 10: DEATH, BE NOT PROUD

by John Donne

Death, be not proud, though some have called thee
Mighty and dreadful, for thou art not so;
For those whom thou think'st thou dost overthrow
Die not, poor Death, nor yet canst thou kill me.
From rest and sleep, which but thy pictures be,
Much pleasure; then from thee much more must flow,
And soonest our best men with thee do go,
Rest of their bones, and soul's delivery.
Thou art slave to fate, chance, kings, and desperate men,
And dost with poison, war, and sickness dwell,
And poppy or charms can make us sleep as well
And better than thy stroke; why swell'st thou then?
One short sleep past, we wake eternally
And death shall be no more; Death, thou shalt die.

NO MAN IS AN ISLAND

by John Donne

No man is an island,
Entire of itself,
Every man is a piece of the continent,
A part of the main.
If a clod be washed away by the sea,
Europe is the less.
As well as if a promontory were.
As well as if a manor of thy friend's
Or of thine own were:
Any man's death diminishes me,
Because I am involved in mankind,
And therefore never send to know for whom the bell tolls;
It tolls for thee.

GO AND CATCH A FALLING STAR

by John Donne

Go and catch a falling star,
    Get with child a mandrake root,
Tell me where all past years are,
    Or who cleft the devil's foot,
Teach me to hear mermaids singing,
Or to keep off envy's stinging,
      And find
      What wind
Serves to advance an honest mind.

If thou be'st born to strange sights,
    Things invisible to see,
Ride ten thousand days and nights,
    Till age snow white hairs on thee,
Thou, when thou return'st, wilt tell me,
All strange wonders that befell thee,
      And swear,
      No where
Lives a woman true, and fair.

If thou find'st one, let me know,
    Such a pilgrimage were sweet;
Yet do not, I would not go,
    Though at next door we might meet;
Though she were true, when you met her,
And last, till you write your letter,
      Yet she
      Will be
False, ere I come, to two, or three.

FOR WHOM THE BELL TOLLS

by John Donne

No man is an island,
Entire of itself.
Each is a piece of the continent,
A part of the main.
If a clod be washed away by the sea,
Europe is the less.
As well as if a promontory were.
As well as if a manor of thine own
Or of thine friend's were.
Each man's death diminishes me,
For I am involved in mankind.
Therefore, send not to know
For whom the bell tolls,
It tolls for thee.

THE CANONIZATION

by John Donne

For God's sake hold your tongue, and let me love,
    Or chide my palsy, or my gout,
    My five grey hairs, or ruin'd fortune flout,
With wealth your state, your mind with arts improve,
      Take you a course, get you a place,
      Observe his Honour, or his Grace,
Or the King's real, or his stampèd face
    Contemplate, what you will, approve,
    So you will let me love.

Alas, alas, who's injur'd by my love?
    What merchant's ships have my sighs drown'd?
    Who says my tears have overflow'd his ground?
When did my colds a forward spring remove?
      When did the heats which my veins fill
      Add one more to the plaguy bill?
Soldiers find wars, and lawyers find out still
    Litigious men, which quarrels move,
    Though she and I do love.

Call us what you will, we are made such by love;
    Call her one, me another fly,
    We'are tapers too, and at our own cost die,
And we in us find the'eagle and the dove.
      The phœnix riddle hath more wit
      By us; we two being one, are it.

So, to one neutral thing both sexes fit,
　　We die and rise the same, and prove
　　Mysterious by this love.

We can die by it, if not live by love,
　　And if unfit for tombs and hearse
　　Our legend be, it will be fit for verse;
And if no piece of chronicle we prove,
　　We'll build in sonnets pretty rooms;
　　As well a well-wrought urn becomes
The greatest ashes, as half-acre tombs,
　　And by these hymns all shall approve
　　Us canoniz'd for love;

And thus invoke us: "You, whom reverend love
　　Made one another's hermitage;
　　You, to whom love was peace, that now is rage;
Who did the whole world's soul contract, and drove
　　Into the glasses of your eyes
　　(So made such mirrors, and such spies,
That they did all to you epitomize)
　　Countries, towns, courts: beg from above
　　A pattern of your love!"

WE WEAR THE MASK

by *Paul Laurence Dunbar*

We wear the mask that grins and lies,
It hides our cheeks and shades our eyes,—
This debt we pay to human guile;
With torn and bleeding hearts we smile,
And mouth with myriad subtleties.

Why should the world be over-wise,
In counting all our tears and sighs?
Nay, let them only see us, while

    We wear the mask.
We smile, but, O great Christ, our cries
To thee from tortured souls arise.
We sing, but oh the clay is vile
Beneath our feet, and long the mile;
But let the world dream otherwise,
    We wear the mask!

THE LOVE SONG OF J. ALFRED PRUFROCK

by T. S. Eliot

S'io credesse che mia risposta fosse
A persona che mai tornasse al mondo,
Questa fiamma staria senza piu scosse.
Ma percioche giammai di questo fondo
Non torno vivo alcun, s'i'odo il vero,
Senza tema d'infamia ti rispondo.

Let us go then, you and I,
When the evening is spread out against the sky
Like a patient etherized upon a table;
Let us go, through certain half-deserted streets,
The muttering retreats
Of restless nights in one-night cheap hotels
And sawdust restaurants with oyster-shells:
Streets that follow like a tedious argument
Of insidious intent
To lead you to an overwhelming question …
Oh, do not ask, "What is it?"
Let us go and make our visit.

In the room the women come and go
Talking of Michelangelo.

The yellow fog that rubs its back upon the window-panes,
The yellow smoke that rubs its muzzle on the window-panes,
Licked its tongue into the corners of the evening,
Lingered upon the pools that stand in drains,
Let fall upon its back the soot that falls from chimneys,
Slipped by the terrace, made a sudden leap,

And seeing that it was a soft October night,
Curled once about the house, and fell asleep.
And indeed there will be time
For the yellow smoke that slides along the street,
Rubbing its back upon the window-panes;
There will be time, there will be time
To prepare a face to meet the faces that you meet;
There will be time to murder and create,
And time for all the works and days of hands
That lift and drop a question on your plate;
Time for you and time for me,
And time yet for a hundred indecisions,
And for a hundred visions and revisions,
Before the taking of a toast and tea.

In the room the women come and go
Talking of Michelangelo.

And indeed there will be time
To wonder, "Do I dare?" and, "Do I dare?"
Time to turn back and descend the stair,
With a bald spot in the middle of my hair —
(They will say: "How his hair is growing thin!")
My morning coat, my collar mounting firmly to the chin,
My necktie rich and modest, but asserted by a simple pin —
(They will say: "But how his arms and legs are thin!")
Do I dare
Disturb the universe?
In a minute there is time
For decisions and revisions which a minute will reverse.

For I have known them all already, known them all:
Have known the evenings, mornings, afternoons,
I have measured out my life with coffee spoons;
I know the voices dying with a dying fall
Beneath the music from a farther room.
        So how should I presume?

And I have known the eyes already, known them all—
The eyes that fix you in a formulated phrase,
And when I am formulated, sprawling on a pin,
When I am pinned and wriggling on the wall,
Then how should I begin
To spit out all the butt-ends of my days and ways?
      And how should I presume?

And I have known the arms already, known them all—
Arms that are braceleted and white and bare
(But in the lamplight, downed with light brown hair!)
Is it perfume from a dress
That makes me so digress?
Arms that lie along a table, or wrap about a shawl.
      And should I then presume?
      And how should I begin?

Shall I say, I have gone at dusk through narrow streets
And watched the smoke that rises from the pipes
Of lonely men in shirt-sleeves, leaning out of windows? ...

I should have been a pair of ragged claws
Scuttling across the floors of silent seas.

And the afternoon, the evening, sleeps so peacefully!
Smoothed by long fingers,
Asleep ... tired ... or it malingers,
Stretched on the floor, here beside you and me.
Should I, after tea and cakes and ices,
Have the strength to force the moment to its crisis?
But though I have wept and fasted, wept and prayed,
Though I have seen my head (grown slightly bald) brought in upon a platter,
I am no prophet — and here's no great matter;
I have seen the moment of my greatness flicker,
And I have seen the eternal Footman hold my coat, and snicker,
And in short, I was afraid.

And would it have been worth it, after all,
After the cups, the marmalade, the tea,
Among the porcelain, among some talk of you and me,
Would it have been worth while,
To have bitten off the matter with a smile,
To have squeezed the universe into a ball
To roll it towards some overwhelming question,
To say: "I am Lazarus, come from the dead,
Come back to tell you all, I shall tell you all"—
If one, settling a pillow by her head
    Should say: "That is not what I meant at all;
    That is not it, at all."

And would it have been worth it, after all,
Would it have been worth while,
After the sunsets and the dooryards and the sprinkled streets,
After the novels, after the teacups, after the skirts that trail along the floor—
And this, and so much more?—
It is impossible to say just what I mean!
But as if a magic lantern threw the nerves in patterns on a screen:
Would it have been worth while
If one, settling a pillow or throwing off a shawl,
And turning toward the window, should say:
    "That is not it at all,
    That is not what I meant, at all."

No! I am not Prince Hamlet, nor was meant to be;
Am an attendant lord, one that will do
To swell a progress, start a scene or two,
Advise the prince; no doubt, an easy tool,
Deferential, glad to be of use,
Politic, cautious, and meticulous;
Full of high sentence, but a bit obtuse;
At times, indeed, almost ridiculous—
Almost, at times, the Fool.

I grow old ... I grow old ...
I shall wear the bottoms of my trousers rolled.

Shall I part my hair behind? Do I dare to eat a peach?
I shall wear white flannel trousers, and walk upon the
beach.
I have heard the mermaids singing, each to each.

I do not think that they will sing to me.

I have seen them riding seaward on the waves
Combing the white hair of the waves blown back
When the wind blows the water white and black.
We have lingered in the chambers of the sea
By sea-girls wreathed with seaweed red and brown
Till human voices wake us, and we drown.

THE WASTE LAND

by T. S. Eliot

Part 1 - *Burial of the Dead*

April is the cruelest month, breeding
Lilacs out of the dead land, mixing
Memory and desire, stirring
Dull roots with spring rain.
Winter kept us warm, covering
Earth in forgetful snow, feeding
A little life with dried tubers.
Summer surprised us, coming over the Starnbergersee
With a shower of rain; we stopped in the colonnade,
And went on in sunlight, into the Hofgarten
And drank coffee, and talked for an hour.
Bin gar keine Russin, stamm' aus Litauen, echt deutsch.
And when we were children, staying at the arch-duke's,
My cousin's, he took me out on a sled,
And I was frightened. He said, Marie,
Marie, hold on tight. And down we went.
In the mountains, there you feel free.
I read, much of the night, and go south in the winter.

What are the roots that clutch, what branches grow
Out of this stony rubbish? Son of man,
You canot say, or guess, for you know only
A heap of broken images, where the sun beats,
And the dead tree gives no shelter, the cricket no relief,

And the dry stone no sound of water. Only
There is shadow under this red rock,
(Come in under the shadow of this red rock),
And I will show you something different from either
your shadow at morning striding behind you
or your shadow at evening rising to meet you;
I will show you fear in a handful of dust.
 Frisch weht der Wind
 Der Heimat zu
 Mein Irisch Kind,
 Wo weilest du?
'You gave me hyacinths first a year ago;
They called me the hyacinth girl.'
—Yet when we came back, late, from the hyacinth garden,
Your arms full and your hair wet, I could not
Speak, and my eyes failed, I was neither
Living nor dead, and I knew nothing,
Looking into the heart of light, the silence.
Oed' und leer das Meer.

Madame Sosostris, famous clairvoyante,
Had a bad cold, nevertheless
Is known to be the wisest woman in Europe,
With a wicked pack of cards. Here, said she,
Is your card, the drowned Phoenician Sailor,
(Those are pearls that were his eyes. Look!)
Here is Belladonna, the Lady of the Rocks,
The lady of situations.
Here is the man with three staves, and here the Wheel,
And here is the one-eyed merchant, and this card,
Which is blank, is something he carries on his back,
Which I am forbidden to see. I do not find
The Hanged Man. Fear death by water.
I see crowds of people, walking round in a ring.
Thank you. If you see dear Mrs. Equitone,
Tell her I bring the horoscope myself:
One must be so careful these days.

Unreal City
Under the brown fog of a winter dawn,
A crowd flowed over London Bridge, so many,
I had not thought death had undone so many.
Sighs, short and infrequent, were exhaled,
And each man fixed his eyes before his feet.
Flowed up the hill and down King William Street,
To where Saint Mary Woolnoth kept the hours
With a dead sound on the final stroke of nine.
There I saw one I knew, and stopped him, crying: 'Stetson!
'You who were with me in the ships at Mylae
'That corpse you planted last year in your garden,
'Has it begun to sprout? Will it bloom this year?
'Or has the sudden frost disturbed its bed?
'O keep the Dog far hence, that's friend to men,
'Or with his nails he'll dig it up again!
'You! hypocrite lecteur!—mon semblable,—mon frere!'

Part 2 - A Game of Chess

The Chair she sat in, like a burnished throne,
Glowed on the marble, where the glass
Held up by standards wrought with fruited vines
From which a golden Cupidon peeped out
(Another hid his eyes behind his wing)
Doubled the flames of seven-branched candleabra
Reflecting light upon the table as
The glitter of her jewels rose to meet it,
From satin cases poured in rich profusion.
In vials of ivory and coloured glass
Unstoppered, lurked her strange synthetic perfume
Unguent, powdered, or liquid—troubled, vondused
And drowned the sense in odours; stirred by the air
That freshened from the window, these ascended
In fattening the prolonged candle-flames,
Flung their smoke into the laquearia,

Stirring the pattern on the coffered ceiling.
Huge sea-wood fed with copper
Burned green and orange, framed by the colored stone
In which sad light a carved dolphin swam
Above the antique mantel was displayed
As though a window gave upon the sylvan scene
The change of Philomel, by the barbarous king
So rudely forced; yet there the nightingale
Filled all the desert with inviolable voice
And still she cried, and still the world pursues,
'Jug Jug' to dirty ears.
And other withered stumps of time
Were told upon the walls; staring forms
Leaned out, leaning, hushing the room enclosed.
Footstpes shuffled on the stair.
Under the firelight, under the brush, her hair
Spread out in fiery points
Glowed into words, then would be savagely still.

'My nerves are bad t-night. Yes, bad. Stay with me.
'Speak to me. Why do you never speak? Speak.
    'What are you thinking of? What thinking? What?
'I never know what you are thinking. Think.'

I think we are in rat's alley
Where the dead men lost their bones.

'What is that noise?'
    The wind under the door.
'What is that noise now? What is the wind doing?'
    Nothing again nothing.

'Do
'You know nothing? Do you see nothing? Do you remember
'Nothing?'
I remember
Those pearls that were his eyes.

'Are you alive, or not? Is there nothing in your head?'
But
O O O O that Shakespeherian Rag—
It's so elegant
So intelligent
'What shall I do now? What shall I do?'
'I shall rush out as I am, walk the street
'With my hair down, so. What shall we do to-morrow?
'What shall we ever do?
    The hot water at ten.
And if it rains, a closed car at four.
And we shall play a game of chess,
Pressing lidless eyes and waiting for a knock upon the door.

When Lil's husband got demobbed, I said—
I didn't mince my words, I said to her myself,
HURRY UP PLEASE ITS TIME
Now Albert's coming back, make yourself a bit smart.
He'll want to know what you done with that money he gave you
To get yourself some teeth. He did, I was there.
You have them all out, Lil, and get a nice set,
He said, I swear, I can't bear to look at you.
And no more can't I, I said, and think of poor Albert,
He's been in the army for four years, he wants a good time
And if you don't give it him, there's others will, I said.
Oh is there, she said. Something o' that, I said.
Then I'll know who to thank, she said, and give me a straight look.
HURRY UP PLEASE ITS TIME
If you don't like it you can get on with it, I said.
Others can pick and choose if you can't.
But if Albert makes off, it won't be for lack of telling.
You ought to be ashamed, I said, to look so antique.
(And her thirty-one.)
I can't help it, she said, pulling a long face,
It's them pills I took, to bring it off, she said.
(She had five already and nearly died of young George.)

The chemist said it would be all right, but I've never been the same.
You are a proper fool, I said.
Well, if Albert won't leave you alone, there it is, I said,
What you get married for if you don't want children?
HURRY UP PLEASE ITS TIME
Well, that Sunday Albert was home, they had a hot gammon
And they asked me in to dinner, to get the beauty of it—
HURRY UP PLEASE ITS TIME
HURRY UP PLEASE ITS TIME
Goodnight Bill. Goodnight Lou. Goodnight May. Goodnight.
Ta ta. Goodnight. Goodnight.
Good night, ladies, good night, sweet ladies, good night, good night.

Part 3 - The Fire Sermon

The river's tent is broken: the last fingers of leaf
Clutch and sink into the wet bank. The wind
Crosses the brown land, unheard. The nymphs are departed.
Sweet Thames, run softly, till I end my song.
The river bears no empty bottles, sandwich papers,
Silk handkerchiefs, cardboard boxes, cigarette ends
Or other testimony of summer nights. The nymphs are departed.
And their friends, the loitering heirs of City directors;
Departed, have left no addresses.
By the waters of Leman I sat down and wept…
Sweet Thames, run softly till I end my song,
Sweet Thames, run softly, for I speak not loud or long.
But at my back in a cold blast I hear
The ratttle of bones, and chuckle spread from ear to ear.

A rat crept softly through vegetation
Dragging its slimy belly on the bank
While I was fishing in the dull canal
On a winter evening round behind the gashouse
Musing upon the king my brother's wreck

And the king my father's death before him.
White bodies naked on the low damp ground
And bones cast in a little low dry garret,
Rattled by the rat's foot only, year to year.
But at my back from time to time I hear
The sound of horns and motors, which shall bring
Sweeney to Mrs. Porter in the spring.
O the moon shone bright on Mrs. Porter
And on her daughter
They wash their feet in soda water
Et O ces voix d'enfants, chantant dans la coupole!

Twit twit twit
Jug jug jug jug jug jug
So rudely forc'd
Tereu

Unreal City
Under the brown fog of a winter noon
Mr. Eugenides, the Smyrna merchant
Unshaven, with a pocket full of currants
C.i.f. London: documents at sight,
Asked me in demotic French
To luncheon at the Cannon Street Hotel
Followed by a weekend at the Metropole.

At the violet hour, when the eyes and back
Turn upward from the desk, when the human engine waits
Like a taxi throbbing waiting,
I Tiresias, though blind, throbbing between two lives,
Old man with wrinkled female breasts, can see
At the violet hour, the evening hour that strives
Homeward, and brings the sailor home from sea,
The typist home at teatime, clears her breakfast, lights
Her stove, and lays out food; in tins.
Out of the window perilously spread

Her drying combinations touched by the sun's last rays,
On the divan are piled (at night her bed)
Stockings, slippers, camisoles, and stays.
I Tiresias, old man with wrinkled dugs
Perceived the scene, and foretold the rest—
I too awaited the expected guest.
He, the young man carbuncular, arrives,
A small house agent's clerk, with one bold stare,
One of the low on whom assurance sits
As a silk hat on a Bradford millionaire.
The time is now propitious, as he guesses,
The meal is ended, she is bored and tired,
Endeavours to engage her in caresses
Which are still unreproved, if undesired.
Flushed and decided, he assaults at one;
Exploring hands rencounter no defence;
His vanity requires no response,
And makes a welcome of indifference.
(And I Tiresias have foresuffered all
Enacted on this same divan or bed;
I who have sat by Thebes below the wall
And walked amongh the lowest of the dead.)
Bestows one final patronising kiss,
And gropes his way, finding the stairs unlit…

She turns and looks a moment in the glass,
Hardly aware of her departed love;
Her brain allows one-half formed thought to pass:
'Well now that's done: and I'm glad it's over.'
When lovely woman stoops to folly and
Paces about her room again, alone,
She smooths her hair with automatic hand,
And puts a record on the gramaphone.

'This music crept by me upon the waters'
And along the Strand, up Queen Victoria Street.
O City city, I can sometimes hear
Beside a public bar in Lower Thames Street,
The pleasant whining of a mandolin
And a clatter and a chatter from within
Where fishmen lounge at noon: where the walls
Of Magnus Martyr hold
Inexplicable splendour of Ionian white and gold.

    The river sweats
    Oil and tar
    The barges drift
    With the turning tide
    Red sails
    Wide
    To leeward, swing on the heavy spar.
    The barges wash
    Drifting logs
    Down Greenwich reach
    Past the Isle of Dogs.
      Weialala leia
      Wallala leialala

    Elizabeth and Leicester
    Beating oars
    The stern was formed
    A gilded shell
    Red and gold
    The brisk swell
    Rippled both shores
    Southwest wind
    Carried down stream

The peal of bells
White towers
  Weialala leia
  Wallala leialala

'Trams and dusty trees
Highbury bore me. Richmond and Kew
Undid me. By Richmond I raised my knees
Supine on the floor of a narrow canoe.'

'My feet are Moorgate, and my heart
Under my feet. After the event
He wept. He promisd "a new start."
I made no comment. What should I resent?'

'On Margate Sands.
I can connect
Nothing with nothing.
The broken fingernails of dirty hands.
My people humble people who expect
Nothing.'
  la la

To Carthage then I came

Burning burning burning burning
O Lord Thou pluckest me out
O Lord Thou pluckest

burning

Part 4 - Death by Water

Phelbas the Phoenician, a fortnight dead,
Forgot the cry of gulls, and the deep sea swell
And the profit and loss.
A current under sea
Picked his bones in whispers. As he rose and fell
He passed the stages of his age and youth
Entering whirpool.
Gentile or Jew
O you who turn the wheel and look to windward,
Consider Phlebas, who was once handsome and tall as you.

Part 5 - What the Thunder Said

After the torchlight red on sweaty faces
After the frosty silence in the gardens
After the agony in stony places
The shouting and the crying
Prison and palace and reverberation
Of thunder of spring over distant mountains
He who was living is now dead
We who were living are now dying
With a little patience

Here is no water but only rock
Rock and no water and the sandy road
The road winding above among the mountains
Which are mountains of rock without water
If there were water we should stop and drink
Amongst the rock one cannot stop or think
Sweat is dry and feet are in the sand
If there were only water amongst the rock
Dead mountain mouth of carious teeth that cannot spit

Here one can neither stand nor lie nor sit
There is not even slience in the mountains
But dry sterile thunder without rain
There is not even solitude in the mountains
But red sullen faces sneer and snarl
From doors of mudcracked houses
        If there were water
And no rock
If there were rock
And also water
And water
A spring
A pool among the rock
If there were the sound of water only
Not the cicada
And dry grass singing
But sound of water over a rock
Where the hermit-thrush sings in the pine trees
Drip drop drip drop drop drop drop
But there is no water

Who is the third who walks always beside you?
When I count, there are only you and I together
But when I look ahead up the white road
There is always another one walking beside you
Gliding wrapt in a brown mantle, hooded
I do not know whether a man or a woman
—But who is that on the other side of you?

What is that sound high in the air
Murmur of maternal lamentation
Why are those hooded hordes swarming
Over endless plains, stumbling in cracked earth
Ringed by the flat horizon only
What is the city over the mountains

Cracks and reforms and burst in the violet air
Falling towers
Jerusalem Athens Alexandria
Vienna London
Unreal

A woman drew her long black hair out tight
And fiddled whisper music on those strings
And bats with baby faces in the violet light
Whistled, and beat their wings
And crawled head downward down a blackened wall
And upsdie down in air were towers
Tolling reminiscent bells, that kept the hours
And voices singing out of empty cisterns and exhausted wells

In this decayed hole among the mountains
In the faint moonlight, the grass is singing
Over the tumbled graves, about the chapel
There is an empty chapel, on the wind's home.
It has no windows, and the door swings,
Dry bones can harm no one.
Only a cock stood on the rooftree
Co co rico co co rico
In a flash of lightning. Then a damp gust
Bringing rain
Ganga was sunken, and the limp leaves
Waited for rain, while the black clouds
Gathered far distant, over Himavant.
The jungle crouched, humped in silence.
Then spoke the thunder
DA
Datta: what have we give?
My friend, blood shaking my heart
The awful daring of a moment's surrender
Which an age of prudence can never retract
By this, and this only, we have existed

Which is not to be found in our obituaries
Or in memories draped by the beneficient spider
Or under seals broken by the lean solicitor
In our empty rooms
DA
Dayadhvam: I have heard the key
Turn in the door once and turn once only
We think of the key, each in his prison
Thinking of the key, each confirms a prison
Only at nightfall, aethereal rumours
Revive for a moment a broken Coriolanus
DA
Damyata: The boat responded
Gaily, to the hand expert with sail and oar
The sea was calm, your heart would have responded
Gaily, when invited, beating obedient
To controlling hands
    I sat upon the shore
Fishing, with arid plain behind me
Shall I at least set my lands in order?
London Bridge is falling down falling down falling down
Poi s'ascose nel foco che gli affina
Quando fiam uti chelidon—O swallow swallow
Le Prince d'Aquitaine a la tour abolie
These fragments I have shored against my ruins
Why then Ile fit you. Hieronymo's mad againe.
Datta. Dayadhvam. Damyata.
  Shantih   Shantih   Shantih

CONCORD HYMN

by Ralph Waldo Emerson

By the rude bridge that arched the flood,
Their flag to April's breeze unfurled,
Here once the embattled farmers stood
And fired the shot heard round the
world.

The foe long since in silence slept;
Alike the conqueror silent sleeps;
And Time the ruined bridge has swept
Down the dark stream which seaward
creeps.

On this green bank, by this soft stream,
We set today a votive stone;
That memory may their deed redeem,
When, like our sires, our sons are gone.

Spirit, that made those heroes dare
To die, and leave their children free,
Bid Time and Nature gently spare
The shaft we raise to them and thee.

THE SNOWSTORM

by *Ralph Waldo Emerson*

Announced by all the trumpets of the sky,
Arrives the snow, and, driving o'er the fields,
Seems nowhere to alight: the whited air
Hides hill and woods, the river, and the
heaven,
And veils the farmhouse at the garden's end.
The sled and traveller stopped, the courier's
feet
Delated, all friends shut out, the housemates
sit
Around the radiant fireplace, enclosed
In a tumultuous privacy of storm.
Come see the north wind's masonry.
Out of an unseen quarry evermore
Furnished with tile, the fierce artificer
Curves his white bastions with projected roof
Round every windward stake, or tree, or
door.
Speeding, the myriad-handed, his wild work
So fanciful, so savage, nought cares he

For number or proportion. Mockingly,
On coop or kennel he hangs Parian wreaths;
A swan-like form invests the hiddden thorn;
Fills up the famer's lane from wall to wall,
Maugre the farmer's sighs; and at the gate
A tapering turret overtops the work.
And when his hours are numbered, and the world
Is all his own, retiring, as he were not,
Leaves, when the sun appears, astonished Art
To mimic in slow structures, stone by stone,
Built in an age, the mad wind's night-work,
The frolic architecture of the snow.

ACQUAINTED WITH THE NIGHT

by Robert Frost

I have been one acquainted with the night.
I have walked out in rain—and back in rain.
I have outwalked the furthest city light.

I have looked down the saddest city lane.
I have passed by the watchman on his beat
And dropped my eyes, unwilling to explain.

I have stood still and stopped the sound of feet
When far away an interrupted cry
Came over houses from another street,

But not to call me back or say good-bye;
And further still at an unearthly height,
One luminary clock against the sky

Proclaimed the time was neither wrong nor right.
I have been one acquainted with the night.

BIRCHES

by Robert Frost

When I see birches bend to left and right
Across the lines of straighter darker trees,
I like to think some boy's been swinging them.
But swinging doesn't bend them down to stay.
Ice-storms do that. Often you must have seen them
Loaded with ice a sunny winter morning
After a rain. They click upon themselves
As the breeze rises, and turn many-colored
As the stir cracks and crazes their enamel.
Soon the sun's warmth makes them shed crystal shells
Shattering and avalanching on the snow-crust—
Such heaps of broken glass to sweep away
You'd think the inner dome of heaven had fallen.
They are dragged to the withered bracken by the load,
And they seem not to break; though once they are bowed
So low for long, they never right themselves:
You may see their trunks arching in the woods
Years afterwards, trailing their leaves on the ground
Like girls on hands and knees that throw their hair
Before them over their heads to dry in the sun.
But I was going to say when Truth broke in
With all her matter-of-fact about the ice-storm
(Now am I free to be poetical?)
I should prefer to have some boy bend them
As he went out and in to fetch the cows—
Some boy too far from town to learn baseball,

Whose only play was what he found himself,
Summer or winter, and could play alone.
One by one he subdued his father's trees
By riding them down over and over again
Until he took the stiffness out of them,
And not one but hung limp, not one was left
For him to conquer. He learned all there was
To learn about not launching out too soon
And so not carrying the tree away
Clear to the ground. He always kept his poise
To the top branches, climbing carefully
With the same pains you use to fill a cup
Up to the brim, and even above the brim.
Then he flung outward, feet first, with a swish,
Kicking his way down through the air to the ground.
So was I once myself a swinger of birches.
And so I dream of going back to be.
It's when I'm weary of considerations,
And life is too much like a pathless wood
Where your face burns and tickles with the cobwebs
Broken across it, and one eye is weeping
From a twig's having lashed across it open.
I'd like to get away from earth awhile
And then come back to it and begin over.
May no fate willfully misunderstand me
And half grant what I wish and snatch me away
Not to return. Earth's the right place for love:
I don't know where it's likely to go better.
I'd like to go by climbing a birch tree,
And climb black branches up a snow-white trunk
Toward heaven, till the tree could bear no more,
But dipped its top and set me down again.
That would be good both going and coming back.
One could do worse than be a swinger of birches.

FIRE AND ICE

by Robert Frost

Some say the world will end in fire,
Some say in ice.
From what I've tasted of desire
I hold with those who favor fire.
But if it had to perish twice,
I think I know enough of hate
To say that for destruction ice
Is also great
And would suffice.

MENDING WALL

by Robert Frost

Something there is that doesn't love a wall,
That sends the frozen-ground-swell under it,
And spills the upper boulders in the sun;
And makes gaps even two can pass abreast.
The work of hunters is another thing:
I have come after them and made repair
Where they have left not one stone on a stone,
But they would have the rabbit out of hiding,
To please the yelping dogs. The gaps I mean,
No one has seen them made or heard them made,
But at spring mending-time we find them there.
I let my neighbour know beyond the hill;
And on a day we meet to walk the line
And set the wall between us once again.
We keep the wall between us as we go.
To each the boulders that have fallen to each.
And some are loaves and some so nearly balls
We have to use a spell to make them balance:
"Stay where you are until our backs are turned!"
We wear our fingers rough with handling them.
Oh, just another kind of out-door game,
One on a side. It comes to little more:
There where it is we do not need the wall:
He is all pine and I am apple orchard.
My apple trees will never get across
And eat the cones under his pines, I tell him.
He only says, "Good fences make good neighbours."
Spring is the mischief in me, and I wonder

If I could put a notion in his head:
"Why do they make good neighbours? Isn't it
Where there are cows? But here there are no cows.
Before I built a wall I'd ask to know
What I was walling in or walling out,
And to whom I was like to give offence.
Something there is that doesn't love a wall,
That wants it down." I could say "Elves" to him,
But it's not elves exactly, and I'd rather
He said it for himself. I see him there
Bringing a stone grasped firmly by the top
In each hand, like an old-stone savage armed.
He moves in darkness as it seems to me,
Not of woods only and the shade of trees.
He will not go behind his father's saying,
And he likes having thought of it so well
He says again, "Good fences make good neighbours."

NOTHING GOLD CAN STAY

by Robert Frost

Nature's first green is gold,
Her hardest hue to hold,

Her early leaf's a flower;
But only so an hour.

Then leaf subsides to leaf.
So Eden sank to grief,

So dawn goes down to day.
Nothing gold can stay.

STOPPING BY WOODS ON A SNOWY EVENING

by Robert Frost

Whose woods these are I think I know.
His house is in the village though;
He will not see me stopping here
To watch his woods fill up with snow.

My little horse must think it queer
To stop without a farmhouse near
Between the woods and frozen lake
The darkest evening of the year.

He gives his harness bells a shake
To ask if there is some mistake.
The only other sound's the sweep
Of easy wind and downy flake.

The woods are lovely, dark and deep.
But I have promises to keep,
And miles to go before I sleep,
And miles to go before I sleep.

THE ROAD NOT TAKEN

by Robert Frost

Two roads diverged in a yellow wood,
And sorry I could not travel both
And be one traveler, long I stood
And looked down one as far as I could
To where it bent in the undergrowth;

Then took the other, as just as fair,
And having perhaps the better claim,
Because it was grassy and wanted wear;
Though as for that the passing there
Had worn them really about the same,

And both that morning equally lay
In leaves no step had trodden black.
Oh, I kept the first for another day!
Yet knowing how way leads on to way,
I doubted if I should ever come back.

I shall be telling this with a sigh
Somewhere ages and ages hence:
Two roads diverged in a wood, and I—
I took the one less traveled by,
And that has made all the difference.

DO NOT STAND AT MY GRAVE AND WEEP

by Mary Frye

Do not stand at my grave and weep;
I am not there. I do not sleep.
I am a thousand winds that blow.
I am the diamond glints on snow.
I am the sunlight on ripened grain.
I am the gentle autumn rain.
When you awaken in the morning's hush
I am the swift uplifting rush
Of quiet birds in circled flight.
I am the soft stars that shine at night.
Do not stand at my grave and cry;
I am not there.
I did not die.

ELEGY WRITTEN IN A COUNTRY CHURCHYARD

by Thomas Gray

The curfew tolls the knell of parting day,
   The lowing herd wind slowly o'er the lea,
The plowman homeward plods his weary way,
   And leaves the world to darkness and to me.

Now fades the glimm'ring landscape on the sight,
   And all the air a solemn stillness holds,
Save where the beetle wheels his droning flight,
   And drowsy tinklings lull the distant folds;

Save that from yonder ivy-mantled tow'r
   The moping owl does to the moon complain
Of such, as wand'ring near her secret bow'r,
   Molest her ancient solitary reign.

Beneath those rugged elms, that yew-tree's shade,
   Where heaves the turf in many a mould'ring heap,
Each in his narrow cell for ever laid,
   The rude forefathers of the hamlet sleep.

The breezy call of incense-breathing Morn,
   The swallow twitt'ring from the straw-built shed,
The cock's shrill clarion, or the echoing horn,
   No more shall rouse them from their lowly bed.

For them no more the blazing hearth shall burn,
   Or busy housewife ply her evening care:

No children run to lisp their sire's return,
   Or climb his knees the envied kiss to share.

Oft did the harvest to their sickle yield,
   Their furrow oft the stubborn glebe has broke;
How jocund did they drive their team afield!
   How bow'd the woods beneath their sturdy stroke!

Let not Ambition mock their useful toil,
   Their homely joys, and destiny obscure;
Nor Grandeur hear with a disdainful smile
   The short and simple annals of the poor.

The boast of heraldry, the pomp of pow'r,
   And all that beauty, all that wealth e'er gave,
Awaits alike th' inevitable hour.
   The paths of glory lead but to the grave.

Nor you, ye proud, impute to these the fault,
   If Mem'ry o'er their tomb no trophies raise,
Where thro' the long-drawn aisle and fretted vault
   The pealing anthem swells the note of praise.

Can storied urn or animated bust
   Back to its mansion call the fleeting breath?
Can Honour's voice provoke the silent dust,
   Or Flatt'ry soothe the dull cold ear of Death?

Perhaps in this neglected spot is laid
   Some heart once pregnant with celestial fire;
Hands, that the rod of empire might have sway'd,
   Or wak'd to ecstasy the living lyre.

But Knowledge to their eyes her ample page
   Rich with the spoils of time did ne'er unroll;
Chill Penury repress'd their noble rage,
   And froze the genial current of the soul.

Full many a gem of purest ray serene,
  The dark unfathom'd caves of ocean bear:
Full many a flow'r is born to blush unseen,
  And waste its sweetness on the desert air.

Some village-Hampden, that with dauntless breast
  The little tyrant of his fields withstood;
Some mute inglorious Milton here may rest,
    Some Cromwell guiltless of his country's blood.

Th' applause of list'ning senates to command,
  The threats of pain and ruin to despise,
To scatter plenty o'er a smiling land,
  And read their hist'ry in a nation's eyes,

Their lot forbade: nor circumscrib'd alone
  Their growing virtues, but their crimes confin'd;
Forbade to wade through slaughter to a throne,
  And shut the gates of mercy on mankind,

The struggling pangs of conscious truth to hide,
  To quench the blushes of ingenuous shame,
Or heap the shrine of Luxury and Pride
  With incense kindled at the Muse's flame.

Far from the madding crowd's ignoble strife,
  Their sober wishes never learn'd to stray;
Along the cool sequester'd vale of life
  They kept the noiseless tenor of their way.

Yet ev'n these bones from insult to protect,
  Some frail memorial still erected nigh,
With uncouth rhymes and shapeless sculpture deck'd,
  Implores the passing tribute of a sigh.

Their name, their years, spelt by th' unletter'd muse,
    The place of fame and elegy supply:
And many a holy text around she strews,
    That teach the rustic moralist to die.

For who to dumb Forgetfulness a prey,
    This pleasing anxious being e'er resign'd,
Left the warm precincts of the cheerful day,
    Nor cast one longing, ling'ring look behind?

On some fond breast the parting soul relies,
    Some pious drops the closing eye requires;
Ev'n from the tomb the voice of Nature cries,
    Ev'n in our ashes live their wonted fires.

For thee, who mindful of th' unhonour'd Dead
    Dost in these lines their artless tale relate;
If chance, by lonely contemplation led,
    Some kindred spirit shall inquire thy fate,

Haply some hoary-headed swain may say,
    "Oft have we seen him at the peep of dawn
Brushing with hasty steps the dews away
    To meet the sun upon the upland lawn.

"There at the foot of yonder nodding beech
    That wreathes its old fantastic roots so high,
His listless length at noontide would he stretch,
    And pore upon the brook that babbles by.

"Hard by yon wood, now smiling as in scorn,
    Mutt'ring his wayward fancies he would rove,
Now drooping, woeful wan, like one forlorn,
    Or craz'd with care, or cross'd in hopeless love.

"One morn I miss'd him on the custom'd hill,
  Along the heath and near his fav'rite tree;
Another came; nor yet beside the rill,
  Nor up the lawn, nor at the wood was he;

"The next with dirges due in sad array
  Slow thro' the church-way path we saw him borne.
Approach and read (for thou canst read) the lay,
  Grav'd on the stone beneath yon aged thorn."

THE EPITAPH

Here rests his head upon the lap of Earth
  A youth to Fortune and to Fame unknown.
Fair Science frown'd not on his humble birth,
  And Melancholy mark'd him for her own.

Large was his bounty, and his soul sincere,
  Heav'n did a recompense as largely send:
He gave to Mis'ry all he had, a tear,
  He gain'd from Heav'n ('twas all he wish'd) a friend.

No farther seek his merits to disclose,
  Or draw his frailties from their dread abode,
(There they alike in trembling hope repose)
  The bosom of his Father and his God.

A FRIEND'S GREETING

by Edgar Albert Guest

I'd like to be the sort of friend
    that you have been to me;
I'd like to be the help that you've been
    always glad to be;
I'd like to mean as much to you
    each minute of the day
As you have meant, old friend of mine,
    to me along the way.

I'd like to do the big things
    and the splendid things for you,
To brush the gray out of your skies
    and leave them only blue;
I'd like to say the kindly things
    that I so oft have heard,
And feel that I could rouse your soul
    the way that mine you've stirred.

I'd like to give back the joy
    that you have given me,
Yet that were wishing you a need
    I hope will never be;
I'd like to make you feel
    as rich as I, who travel on
Undaunted in the darkest hours
    with you to lean upon.

I'm wishing at this Christmas time
   that I could but repay
A portion of the gladness
   that you've strewn along the way;
And could I have one wish this year,
   this only would it be:
I'd like to be the sort of friend
   that you have been to me.

BEING BRAVE AT NIGHT

by Edgar Albert Guest

The other night 'bout two o'clock, or maybe it was three,
An elephant with shining tusks came chasing after me.
His trunk was wavin' in the air an' spoutin' jets of steam
An' he was out to eat me up, but still I didn't scream
Or let him see that I was scared - a better thought I had,
I just escaped from where I was and crawled in bed with Dad.

One time there was a giant who was horrible to see,
He had three heads and twenty arms, an' he came after me
And red hot fire came from his mouths and every hand was red
And he declared he'd grind my bones and make them into bread.
But I was just too smart for him, I fooled him mighty bad,
Before his hands could collar me I crawled in bed with Dad.

I ain't scared of nothin' that comes pesterin' me at night.
Once I was chased by forty ghosts all shimmery an' white.
An' I just raced 'em round the room an' let 'em think maybe
I'd have to stop an' rest awhile, when they could capture me.
Then when they leapt onto my bed, Oh Gee! But they were mad
To find that I had slipped away an' crawled in bed with Dad.

No giants, ghosts or elephants have dared to come in there
'Coz if they did he'd beat 'em up and chase 'em to their lair.
They just hang 'round the children's rooms
an' snap an' snarl an' bite
An' laugh if they can make 'em yell
for help with all their might.
But I don't ever yell out loud. I'm not that sort of lad,
I slip from out the covers and I crawl in bed with Dad.

HAVE YOU EARNED YOUR TOMORROW

by Edgar Albert Guest

Is anybody happier because you passed his way?
    Does anyone remember that you spoke to him today?
This day is almost over, and its toiling time is through;
    Is there anyone to utter now a kindly word of you?

Did you give a cheerful greeting to the friend who came along?
Or a churlish sort of "Howdy" and then vanish in the throng?
Were you selfish pure and simple as you rushed along the way,
Or is someone mighty grateful for a deed you did today?

Can you say tonight, in parting with the day that's slipping fast,
    That you helped a single brother of the many that you passed?
Is a single heart rejoicing over what you did or said;
    Does a man whose hopes were fading now with courage look ahead?

Did you waste the day, or lose it, was it well or sorely spent?
    Did you leave a trail of kindness or a scar of discontent?
As you close your eyes in slumber do you think that God would say,
    You have earned one more tomorrow by the work you did today?

IT COULDN'T BE DONE
by Edgar Albert Guest

Somebody said that it couldn't be done,
    But, he with a chuckle replied
That "maybe it couldn't," but he would be one
    Who wouldn't say so till he'd tried.
So he buckled right in with the trace of a grin
    On his face. If he worried he hid it.
He started to sing as he tackled the thing
    That couldn't be done, and he did it.

Somebody scoffed: "Oh, you'll never do that;
    At least no one has done it";
But he took off his coat and he took off his hat,
    And the first thing we knew he'd begun it.
With a lift of his chin and a bit of a grin,
    Without any doubting or quiddit,
He started to sing as he tackled the thing
    That couldn't be done, and he did it.

There are thousands to tell you it cannot be done,
    There are thousands to prophesy failure;
There are thousands to point out to you one by one,
    The dangers that wait to assail you.
But just buckle it in with a bit of a grin,
    Just take off your coat and go to it;
Just start to sing as you tackle the thing
    That "couldn't be done," and you'll do it.

SEE IT THROUGH

by *Edgar Albert Guest*

When you're up against a trouble,
  Meet it squarely, face to face;
    Lift your chin and set your shoulders,
    Plant your feet and take a brace.
When it's vain to try to dodge it,
  Do the best that you can do;
  You may fail, but you may conquer,
  See it through!

  Black may be the clouds about you
  And your future may seem grim,
But don't let your nerve desert you;
  Keep yourself in fighting trim.
If the worst is bound to happen,
  Spite of all that you can do,
Running from it will not save you,
  See it through!

Even hope may seem but futile,
  When with troubles you're beset,
But remember you are facing
  Just what other men have met.
You may fail, but fall still fighting;
  Don't give up, whate'er you do;
Eyes front, head high to the finish.
  See it through!

THE STICK-TOGETHER FAMILIES

by Edgar Albert Guest

The stick-together families are happier by far
Than the brothers and the sisters who take separate highways are.
The gladdest people living are the wholesome folks who make
A circle at the fireside that no power but death can break.
And the finest of conventions ever held beneath the sun
Are the little family gatherings when the busy day is done.

There are rich folk, there are poor folk, who imagine they are wise,
And they're very quick to shatter all the little family ties.
Each goes searching after pleasure in his own selected way,
Each with strangers likes to wander, and with strangers likes to play.
But it's bitterness they harvest, and it's empty joy they find,
For the children that are wisest are the stick-together kind.

There are some who seem to fancy that for gladness they must roam,
That for smiles that are the brightest they must wander far from home.
That the strange friend is the true friend, and they travel far astray
they waste their lives in striving for a joy that's far away,
But the gladdest sort of people, when the busy day is done,
Are the brothers and the sisters who together share their fun.

It's the stick-together family that wins the joys of earth,
That hears the sweetest music and that finds the finest mirth;
It's the old home roof that shelters all the charm that life can give;
There you find the gladdest play-ground, there the happiest spot to live.
And, O weary, wandering brother, if contentment you would win,
Come you back unto the fireside and be comrade with your kin.

CASABIANCA

by Felicia Hemans

The boy stood on the burning deck,
    Whence all but him had fled;
The flame that lit the battle's wreck
    Shone round him o'er the dead.
Yet beautiful and bright he stood,
    As born to rule the storm;
A creature of heroic blood,
    A proud though childlike form.
The flames rolled on—he would not go
    Without his father's word;
That father, faint in death below,
    His voice no longer heard.
He called aloud, "Say, father, say
    If yet my task is done?"
He knew not that the chieftain lay
    Unconscious of his son.
"Speak, father!" once again he cried,
    "If I may yet be gone!"
And but the booming shots replied,
    And fast the flames rolled on.
Upon his brow he felt their breath,
    And in his waving hair;
And looked from that lone post of death
    In still, yet brave despair.

And shouted but once more aloud
  "My father! must I stay?"
While o'er him fast, through sail and
shroud,
  The wreathing fires made way.
They wrapt the ship in splendour wild,
  They caught the flag on high,
And streamed above the gallant child
  Like banners in the sky.
Then came a burst of thunder sound—
  The boy—oh! where was he?
—Ask of the winds that far around
  With fragments strew the sea;
With mast, and helm, and pennon fair.
  That well had borne their part—
But the noblest thing that perished there
  Was that young, faithful heart.

INVICTUS

by William Ernest Henley

Out of the night that covers me,
 Black as the pit from pole to pole,
I thank whatever gods may be
 For my unconquerable soul.

In the fell clutch of circumstance
 I have not winced nor cried aloud.
Under the bludgeonings of chance
 My head is bloody, but unbowed.

Beyond this place of wrath and tears
 Looms but the Horror of the shade,
And yet the menace of the years
 Finds and shall find me unafraid.

It matters not how strait the gate,
 How charged with punishments the scroll,
I am the master of my fate,
 I am the captain of my soul.

OLD IRONSIDES

by Oliver Wendell Holmes

Ay, tear her tattered ensign down!
   Long has it waved on high,
And many an eye has danced to see
   That banner in the sky;
Beneath it rung the battle shout,
   And burst the cannon's roar;—
The meteor of the ocean air
   Shall sweep the clouds no more!

Her deck, once red with heroes' blood
   Where knelt the vanquished foe,
When winds were hurrying o'er the flood
   And waves were white below,
No more shall feel the victor's tread,
   Or know the conquered knee;—
The harpies of the shore shall pluck
   The eagle of the sea!

O, better that her shattered hulk
   Should sink beneath the wave;
Her thunders shook the mighty deep,
   And there should be her grave;
Nail to the mast her holy flag,
   Set every thread-bare sail,
And give her to the god of storms,—
   The lightning and the gale!

THE CHAMBERED NAUTILUS

by Oliver Wendell Holmes

This is the ship of pearl, which, poets feign,
This is the ship of pearl, which, poets feign,
   Sails the unshadowed main,—
The venturous bark that flings
   On the sweet summer wind its purpled wings
In gulfs enchanted, where the Siren sings,
   And coral reefs lie bare,
Where the cold sea-maids rise to sun their streaming hair.
Its webs of living gauze no more unfurl;
   Wrecked is the ship of pearl!
And every chambered cell,
   Where its dim dreaming life was wont to dwell,
As the frail tenant shaped his growing shell,
   Before thee lies revealed,—
Its irised ceiling rent, its sunless crypt unsealed!
Year after year beheld the silent toil
   That spread his lustrous coil;
Still, as the spiral grew,
   He left the past year's dwelling for the new,
Stole with soft step its shining archway through,
   Built up its idle door,
Stretched in his last-found home, and knew the old no more.
Thanks for the heavenly message brought by thee,
   Child of the wandering sea,
Cast from her lap, forlorn!
   From thy dead lips a clearer note is born

Than ever Triton blew from wreathèd horn!
　　While on mine ear it rings,
Through the deep caves of thought I hear a voice that sings:—
Build thee more stately mansions, O my soul,
　　As the swift seasons roll!
Leave thy low-vaulted past!
　　Let each new temple, nobler than the last,
Shut thee from heaven with a dome more vast,
　　Till thou at length art free,
Leaving thine outgrown shell by life's unresting sea!

GOD'S GRANDEUR

by *Gerard Manley Hopkins*

The world is charged with the grandeur of God.
    It will flame out, like shining from shook foil;
    It gathers to a greatness, like the ooze of oil
Crushed. Why do men then now not reck his rod?
Generations have trod, have trod, have trod;
    And all is seared with trade; bleared, smeared with toil;
    And wears man's smudge and shares man's smell: the soil
Is bare now, nor can foot feel, being shod.

And for all this, nature is never spent;
    There lives the dearest freshness deep down things;
And though the last lights off the black West went
    Oh, morning, at the brown brink eastward, springs—
Because the Holy Ghost over the bent
    World broods with warm breast and with ah! bright wings.

THE WINDHOVER

by Gerard Manley Hopkins

I caught this morning morning's minion, king-
 dom of daylight's dauphin, dapple-dawn-drawn Falcon, in his riding
 Of the rolling level underneath him steady air, and striding
High there, how he rung upon the rein of a wimpling wing
In his ecstasy! then off, off forth on swing,
 As a skate's heel sweeps smooth on a bow-bend: the hurl and gliding
 Rebuffed the big wind. My heart in hiding
Stirred for a bird,—the achieve of; the mastery of the thing!

Brute beauty and valour and act, oh, air, pride, plume, here
 Buckle! AND the fire that breaks from thee then, a billion
Times told lovelier, more dangerous, O my chevalier!

 No wonder of it: shéer plód makes plough down sillion
Shine, and blue-bleak embers, ah my dear,
 Fall, gall themselves, and gash gold-vermillion.

MOTHER TO SON

by James Langston Hughes

Well, son, I'll tell you:
Life for me ain't been no crystal stair.
It's had tacks in it,
And splinters,
And boards torn up,
And places with no carpet on the floor—
Bare.
But all the time
I'se been a-climbin' on,
And reachin' landin's,
And turnin' corners,
And sometimes goin' in the dark
Where there ain't been no light.
So boy, don't you turn back.
Don't you set down on the steps
'Cause you finds it's kinder hard.
Don't you fall now—
For I'se still goin', honey,
I'se still climbin',
And life for me ain't been no crystal stair.

AS I GREW OLDER

by James Langston Hughes

It was a long time ago.
I have almost forgotten my dream.
But it was there then,
In front of me,
Bright like a sun—
My dream.
And then the wall rose,
Rose slowly,
Slowly,
Between me and my dream.
Rose until it touched the sky—
The wall.
Shadow.
I am black.
I lie down in the shadow.
No longer the light of my dream before me,
Above me.
Only the thick wall.
Only the shadow.
My hands!
My dark hands!
Break through the wall!
Find my dream!
Help me to shatter this darkness,
To smash this night,
To break this shadow
Into a thousand lights of sun,
Into a thousand whirling dreams
Of sun!

ABOU BEN ADHEM

by Leigh Hunt

Abou Ben Adhem (may his tribe increase!)
Awoke one night from a deep dream of peace,
And saw, within the moonlight in his room,
Making it rich, and like a lily in bloom,
An angel writing in a book of gold:—
Exceeding peace had made Ben Adhem bold,
And to the presence in the room he said,
"What writest thou?"—The vision raised its head,
And with a look made of all sweet accord,
Answered, "The names of those who love the Lord."
"And is mine one?" said Abou. "Nay, not so,"
Replied the angel. Abou spoke more low,
But cheerly still; and said, "I pray thee, then,
Write me as one that loves his fellow men."

   The angel wrote, and vanished. The next night
It came again with a great wakening light,
And showed the names whom love of God had blest,
And lo! Ben Adhem's name led all the rest.

BRIGHT STAR

by John Keats

Bright star! would I were steadfast as thou art—
   Not in lone splendour hung aloft the night,
And watching, with eternal lids apart,
   Like nature's patient sleepless Eremite,
The moving waters at their priestlike task
   Of pure ablution round earth's human shores,
Or gazing on the new soft fallen mask
   Of snow upon the mountains and the moors—
No—yet still stedfast, still unchangeable,
   Pillow'd upon my fair love's ripening breast,
To feel for ever its soft fall and swell,
   Awake for ever in a sweet unrest,
Still, still to hear her tender-taken breath,
   And so live ever—or else swoon to death.

ENDYMION (EXCERPT)

by John Keats

BOOK I

A thing of beauty is a joy for ever:
Its loveliness increases; it will never
Pass into nothingness; but still will keep
A bower quiet for us, and a sleep
Full of sweet dreams, and health, and quiet breathing.
Therefore, on every morrow, are we wreathing
A flowery band to bind us to the earth,
Spite of despondence, of the inhuman dearth
Of noble natures, of the gloomy days,
Of all the unhealthy and o'er-darkened ways
Made for our searching: yes, in spite of all,
Some shape of beauty moves away the pall
From our dark spirits. Such the sun, the moon,
Trees old and young, sprouting a shady boon
For simple sheep; and such are daffodils
With the green world they live in; and clear rills
That for themselves a cooling covert make
'Gainst the hot season; the mid forest brake,
Rich with a sprinkling of fair musk-rose blooms:
And such too is the grandeur of the dooms
We have imagined for the mighty dead;
All lovely tales that we have heard or read:
An endless fountain of immortal drink,
Pouring unto us from the heaven's brink.

      Nor do we merely feel these essences
For one short hour; no, even as the trees
That whisper round a temple become soon

Dear as the temple's self, so does the moon,
The passion poesy, glories infinite,
Haunt us till they become a cheering light
Unto our souls, and bound to us so fast,
That, whether there be shine, or gloom o'ercast;
They always must be with us, or we die.

        Therefore, 'tis with full happiness that I
Will trace the story of Endymion.
The very music of the name has gone
Into my being, and each pleasant scene
Is growing fresh before me as the green
Of our own valleys: so I will begin
Now while I cannot hear the city's din;
Now while the early budders are just new,
And run in mazes of the youngest hue
About old forests; while the willow trails
Its delicate amber; and the dairy pails
Bring home increase of milk. And, as the year
Grows lush in juicy stalks, I'll smoothly steer
My little boat, for many quiet hours,
With streams that deepen freshly into bowers.
Many and many a verse I hope to write,
Before the daisies, vermeil rimm'd and white,
Hide in deep herbage; and ere yet the bees
Hum about globes of clover and sweet peas,
I must be near the middle of my story.
O may no wintry season, bare and hoary,
See it half finish'd: but let Autumn bold,
With universal tinge of sober gold,
Be all about me when I make an end.
And now, at once adventuresome, I send
My herald thought into a wilderness:
There let its trumpet blow, and quickly dress
My uncertain path with green, that I may speed
Easily onward, thorough flowers and weed.

ODE ON A GRECIAN URN

by John Keats

Thou still unravish'd bride of quietness,
　　Thou foster-child of silence and slow time,
Sylvan historian, who canst thus express
　　A flowery tale more sweetly than our rhyme:
What leaf-fring'd legend haunts about thy shape
　　Of deities or mortals, or of both,
In Tempe or the dales of Arcady?
　　What men or gods are these? What maidens loth?
What mad pursuit? What struggle to escape?
　　What pipes and timbrels? What wild ecstasy?

　　What men or gods are these? What maidens loth?
What mad pursuit? What struggle to escape?
　　What pipes and timbrels? What wild ecstasy?
Heard melodies are sweet, but those unheard
　　Are sweeter; therefore, ye soft pipes, play on;
Not to the sensual ear, but, more endear'd,
　　Pipe to the spirit ditties of no tone:
Fair youth, beneath the trees, thou canst not leave
　　Thy song, nor ever can those trees be bare;
Bold Lover, never, never canst thou kiss,
　　Though winning near the goal yet, do not grieve;
She cannot fade, though thou hast not thy bliss,
　　For ever wilt thou love, and she be fair!

Ah, happy, happy boughs! that cannot shed
　　Your leaves, nor ever bid the Spring adieu;

And, happy melodist, unwearied,
    For ever piping songs for ever new;
More happy love! more happy, happy love!
    For ever warm and still to be enjoy'd,
For ever panting, and for ever young;
    All breathing human passion far above,
That leaves a heart high-sorrowful and cloy'd,
    A burning forehead, and a parching tongue.

Who are these coming to the sacrifice?
    To what green altar, O mysterious priest,
Lead'st thou that heifer lowing at the skies,
    And all her silken flanks with garlands drest?
What little town by river or sea shore,
    Or mountain-built with peaceful citadel,
Is emptied of this folk, this pious morn?
    And, little town, thy streets for evermore
Will silent be; and not a soul to tell
    Why thou art desolate, can e'er return.

O Attic shape! Fair attitude! with brede
    Of marble men and maidens overwrought,
With forest branches and the trodden weed;
    Thou, silent form, dost tease us out of thought
As doth eternity: Cold Pastoral!
    When old age shall this generation waste,
Thou shalt remain, in midst of other woe
    Than ours, a friend to man, to whom thou say'st,
"Beauty is truth, truth beauty,—that is all
    Ye know on earth, and all ye need to know."

ODE TO A NIGHTINGALE

by John Keats

My heart aches, and a drowsy numbness pains
    My sense, as though of hemlock I had drunk,
Or emptied some dull opiate to the drains
    One minute past, and Lethe-wards had sunk:
'Tis not through envy of thy happy lot,
    But being too happy in thy happiness,—
        That thou, light-winged Dryad of the trees,
           In some melodious plot
Of beechen green, and shadows numberless,
    Singest of summer in full-throated ease.

O for a draught of vintage, that hath been
    Cooled a long age in the deep-delved earth,
Tasting of Flora and the country green,
    Dance, and Provençal song, and sunburnt mirth!
O for a beaker full of the warm South,
    Full of the true, the blushful Hippocrene,
        With beaded bubbles winking at the brim,
           And purple-stained mouth;
That I might drink, and leave the world unseen,
    And with thee fade away into the forest dim:

Fade far away, dissolve, and quite forget
    What thou among the leaves hast never known,
The weariness, the fever, and the fret,
    Here, where men sit and hear each other groan;

Where palsy shakes a few, sad, last gray hairs,
   Where youth grows pale, and specter-thin, and dies;
   Where but to think is to be full of sorrow
     And leaden-eyed despairs;
   Where Beauty cannot keep her lustrous eyes,
    Or new Love pine at them beyond to-morrow.

Away! away! for I will fly to thee,
   Not charioted by Bacchus and his pards,
But on the viewless wings of Poesy,
   Though the dull brain perplexes and retards:
Already with thee! tender is the night,
   And haply the Queen-Moon is on her throne,
    Clustered around by all her starry Fays;
     But here there is no light,
Save what from heaven is with the breezes blown
   Through verdurous glooms and winding mossy ways

I cannot see what flowers are at my feet,
   Nor what soft incense hangs upon the boughs,
But, in embalmed darkness, guess each sweet
   Wherewith the seasonable month endows
The grass, the thicket, and the fruit-tree wild;
   White hawthorn, and the pastoral eglantine;
    Fast-fading violets covered up in leaves;
     And mid-May's eldest child,
The coming musk-rose, full of dewy wine,
   The murmurous haunt of flies on summer eves.

Darkling I listen; and, for many a time
   I have been half in love with easeful Death,
Called him soft names in many a mused rhyme,
   To take into the air my quiet breath;
Now more than ever seems it rich to die,
   To cease upon the midnight with no pain,
    While thou art pouring forth thy soul abroad
    In such an ecstasy!

Still wouldst thou sing, and I have ears in vain—
    To thy high requiem become a sod.

Thou wast not born for death, immortal Bird!
    No hungry generations tread thee down;
The voice I hear this passing night was heard
    In ancient days by emperor and clown:
Perhaps the self-same song that found a path
    Through the sad heart of Ruth, when, sick for home,
      She stood in tears amid the alien corn;
        The same that oft-times hath
Charmed magic casements, opening on the foam
    Of perilous seas, in faery lands forlorn.

Forlorn! the very word is like a bell
    To toll me back from thee to my sole self!
Adieu! the fancy cannot cheat so well
    As she is famed to do, deceiving elf.
Adieu! adieu! thy plaintive anthem fades
    Past the near meadows, over the still stream,
      Up the hill-side; and now 'tis buried deep
      In the next valley-glades:
Was it a vision, or a waking dream?
    Fled is that music:—Do I wake or sleep?

TO AUTUMN

by John Keats

Season of mists and mellow fruitfulness,
    Close bosom-friend of the maturing sun;
Conspiring with him how to load and bless
    With fruit the vines that round the thatch-eves run;
To bend with apples the moss'd cottage-trees,
    And fill all fruit with ripeness to the core;
To swell the gourd, and plump the hazel shells
    With a sweet kernel; to set budding more,
And still more, later flowers for the bees,
Until they think warm days will never cease,
    For summer has o'er-brimm'd their clammy cells.

Who hath not seen thee oft amid thy store?
    Sometimes whoever seeks abroad may find
Thee sitting careless on a granary floor,
    Thy hair soft-lifted by the winnowing wind;
Or on a half-reap'd furrow sound asleep,
    Drows'd with the fume of poppies, while thy hook
      Spares the next swath and all its twined flowers:
And sometimes like a gleaner thou dost keep
    Steady thy laden head across a brook;
    Or by a cyder-press, with patient look,
      Thou watchest the last oozings hours by hours.

Where are the songs of spring? Ay, Where are they?
   Think not of them, thou hast thy music too,—
While barred clouds bloom the soft-dying day,
   And touch the stubble-plains with rosy hue;
Then in a wailful choir the small gnats mourn
   Among the river sallows, borne aloft
      Or sinking as the light wind lives or dies;
And full-grown lambs loud bleat from hilly bourn;
   Hedge-crickets sing; and now with treble soft
   The red-breast whistles from a garden-croft;
      And gathering swallows twitter in the skies.

WHEN I HAVE FEARS THAT I MAY CEASE TO BE

by John Keats

When I have fears that I may cease to be
    Before my pen has gleaned my teeming brain,
Before high-pilèd books, in charactery,
    Hold like rich garners the full ripened grain;
When I behold, upon the night's starred face,
    Huge cloudy symbols of a high romance,
And think that I may never live to trace
    Their shadows with the magic hand of chance;
And when I feel, fair creature of an hour,
    That I shall never look upon thee more,
Never have relish in the faery power
    Of unreflecting love—then on the shore
Of the wide world I stand alone, and think
Till love and fame to nothingness do sink.

TREES

by Joyce Kilmer

I think that I shall never see
A poem lovely as a tree.

A tree whose hungry mouth is prest
Against the earth's sweet flowing breast;

A tree that looks at God all day,
And lifts her leafy arms to pray;

A tree that may in Summer wear
A nest of robins in her hair;

Upon whose bosom snow has lain;
Who intimately lives with rain.

Poems are made by fools like me,
But only God can make a tree.

A CHILD'S GARDEN

by Rudyard Kipling

Now there is nothing wrong with me
Except -- I think it's called T.B.
And that is why I have to lay
Out in the garden all the day.

Our garden is not very wide
And cars go by on either side,
And make an angry-hooty noise
That rather startles little boys.

But worst of all is when they take
Me out in cars that growl and shake,
With charabancs so dreadful-near
I have to shut my eyes for fear.

But when I'm on my back again,
I watch the Croydon aeroplane
That flies across to France, and sings
Like hitting thick piano-strings.

When I am strong enough to do
The things I'm truly wishful to,
I'll never use a car or train
But always have an aeroplane;

And just go zooming round and round,
And frighten Nursey with the sound,
And see the angel-side of clouds,
And spit on all those motor-crowds!

IF—

by Rudyard Kipling

If you can keep your head when all about you
    Are losing theirs and blaming it on you,
If you can trust yourself when all men doubt you,
    But make allowance for their doubting too;
If you can wait and not be tired by waiting,
    Or being lied about, don't deal in lies,
Or being hated, don't give way to hating,
    And yet don't look too good, nor talk too wise:

If you can dream—and not make dreams your master;
    If you can think—and not make thoughts your aim;
If you can meet with Triumph and Disaster
    And treat those two impostors just the same;
If you can bear to hear the truth you've spoken
    Twisted by knaves to make a trap for fools,
Or watch the things you gave your life to, broken,
    And stoop and build 'em up with worn-out tools:

If you can make one heap of all your winnings
    And risk it on one turn of pitch-and-toss,
And lose, and start again at your beginnings
    And never breathe a word about your loss;
If you can force your heart and nerve and sinew
    To serve your turn long after they are gone,
And so hold on when there is nothing in you
    Except the Will which says to them: 'Hold on!'

If you can talk with crowds and keep your virtue,
　Or walk with Kings—nor lose the common touch,
If neither foes nor loving friends can hurt you,
　If all men count with you, but none too much;
If you can fill the unforgiving minute
　With sixty seconds' worth of distance run,
Yours is the Earth and everything that's in it,
　And—which is more—you'll be a Man, my son!

RECESSIONAL (A VICTORIAN ODE)

by Rudyard Kipling

God of our fathers, known of old,
   Lord of our far-flung battle-line,
Beneath whose awful Hand we hold
   Dominion over palm and pine—
Lord God of Hosts, be with us yet,
Lest we forget—lest we forget!

The tumult and the shouting dies;
   The Captains and the Kings depart:
Still stands Thine ancient sacrifice,
   An humble and a contrite heart.
Lord God of Hosts, be with us yet,
Lest we forget—lest we forget!

Far-called, our navies melt away;
   On dune and headland sinks the fire:
Lo, all our pomp of yesterday
   Is one with Nineveh and Tyre!
Judge of the Nations, spare us yet,
Lest we forget—lest we forget!

If, drunk with sight of power, we loose
   Wild tongues that have not Thee in awe,
Such boastings as the Gentiles use,
   Or lesser breeds without the Law—
Lord God of Hosts, be with us yet,
Lest we forget—lest we forget!

For heathen heart that puts her trust
   In reeking tube and iron shard,
All valiant dust that builds on dust,
   And guarding, calls not Thee to guard,
For frantic boast and foolish word—
Thy mercy on Thy People, Lord!

THE NEW COLOSSUS

by Emma Lazarus

Not like the brazen giant of Greek fame,
With conquering limbs astride from land to land;
Here at our sea-washed, sunset gates shall stand
A mighty woman with a torch, whose flame
Is the imprisoned lightning, and her name
Mother of Exiles. From her beacon-hand
Glows world-wide welcome; her mild eyes command
The air-bridged harbor that twin cities frame.
"Keep, ancient lands, your storied pomp!" cries she
With silent lips. "Give me your tired, your poor,
Your huddled masses yearning to breathe free,
The wretched refuse of your teeming shore.
Send these, the homeless, tempest-tost to me,
I lift my lamp beside the golden door!"

PAUL REVERE'S RIDE

by Henry Wadsworth Longfellow

Listen, my children, and you shall hear
Of the midnight ride of Paul Revere,
On the eighteenth of April, in Seventy-five;
Hardly a man is now alive
Who remembers that famous day and year.

He said to his friend, "If the British march
By land or sea from the town to-night,
Hang a lantern aloft in the belfry arch
Of the North Church tower as a signal light,--
One, if by land, and two, if by sea;
And I on the opposite shore will be,
Ready to ride and spread the alarm
Through every Middlesex village and farm,
For the country folk to be up and to arm."

Then he said, "Good night!" and with muffled oar
Silently rowed to the Charlestown shore,
Just as the moon rose over the bay,
Where swinging wide at her moorings lay
The Somerset, British man-of-war;
A phantom ship, with each mast and spar
Across the moon like a prison bar,
And a huge black hulk, that was magnified
By its own reflection in the tide.

Meanwhile, his friend, through alley and street,
Wanders and watches with eager ears,
Till in the silence around him he hears
The muster of men at the barrack door,
The sound of arms, and the tramp of feet,
And the measured tread of the grenadiers,
Marching down to their boats on the shore.

Then he climbed the tower of the Old North Church,
By the wooden stairs, with stealthy tread,
To the belfry-chamber overhead,
And startled the pigeons from their perch
On the sombre rafters, that round him made
Masses and moving shapes of shade,--
By the trembling ladder, steep and tall,
To the highest window in the wall,
Where he paused to listen and look down
A moment on the roofs of the town,
And the moonlight flowing over all.

Beneath, in the churchyard, lay the dead,
In their night-encampment on the hill,
Wrapped in silence so deep and still
That he could hear, like a sentinel's tread,
The watchful night-wind, as it went
Creeping along from tent to tent,
And seeming to whisper, "All is well!"
A moment only he feels the spell
Of the place and the hour, and the secret dread
Of the lonely belfry and the dead;
For suddenly all his thoughts are bent
On a shadowy something far away,
Where the river widens to meet the bay,--
A line of black that bends and floats
On the rising tide, like a bridge of boats.

Meanwhile, impatient to mount and ride,
Booted and spurred, with a heavy stride
On the opposite shore walked Paul Revere.
Now he patted his horse's side,
Now gazed at the landscape far and near,
Then, impetuous, stamped the earth,
And turned and tightened his saddle girth;
But mostly he watched with eager search
The belfry-tower of the Old North Church,
As it rose above the graves on the hill,
Lonely and spectral and sombre and still.
And lo! as he looks, on the belfry's height
A glimmer, and then a gleam of light!
He springs to the saddle, the bridle he turns,
But lingers and gazes, till full on his sight
A second lamp in the belfry burns!

A hurry of hoofs in a village street,
A shape in the moonlight, a bulk in the dark,
And beneath, from the pebbles, in passing, a spark
Struck out by a steed flying fearless and fleet:
That was all! And yet, through the gloom and the light,
The fate of a nation was riding that night;
And the spark struck out by that steed, in his flight,
Kindled the land into flame with its heat.

He has left the village and mounted the steep,
And beneath him, tranquil and broad and deep,
Is the Mystic, meeting the ocean tides;
And under the alders, that skirt its edge,
Now soft on the sand, now loud on the ledge,
Is heard the tramp of his steed as he rides.

It was twelve by the village clock,
When he crossed the bridge into Medford town.
He heard the crowing of the cock,
And the barking of the farmer's dog,
And felt the damp of the river fog,
That rises after the sun goes down.

It was one by the village clock,
When he galloped into Lexington.
He saw the gilded weathercock
Swim in the moonlight as he passed,
And the meeting-house windows, blank and bare,
Gaze at him with a spectral glare,
As if they already stood aghast
At the bloody work they would look upon.

It was two by the village clock,
When he came to the bridge in Concord town.
He heard the bleating of the flock,
And the twitter of birds among the trees,
And felt the breath of the morning breeze
Blowing over the meadows brown.
And one was safe and asleep in his bed
Who at the bridge would be first to fall,
Who that day would be lying dead,
Pierced by a British musket-ball.

You know the rest. In the books you have read,
How the British Regulars fired and fled,--
How the farmers gave them ball for ball,
From behind each fence and farm-yard wall,
Chasing the red-coats down the lane,
Then crossing the fields to emerge again
Under the trees at the turn of the road,
And only pausing to fire and load.

So through the night rode Paul Revere;
And so through the night went his cry of alarm
To every Middlesex village and farm,--
A cry of defiance and not of fear,
A voice in the darkness, a knock at the door,
And a word that shall echo forevermore!
For, borne on the night-wind of the Past,
Through all our history, to the last,
In the hour of darkness and peril and need,
The people will waken and listen to hear
The hurrying hoof-beats of that steed,
And the midnight message of Paul Revere.

THE ARROW AND THE SONG

by Henry Wadsworth Longfellow

I shot an arrow into the air,
It fell to earth, I knew not where;
For, so swiftly it flew, the sight
Could not follow it in its flight.

I breathed a song into the air,
It fell to earth, I knew not where;
For who has sight so keen and strong,
That it can follow the flight of song?

Long, long afterward, in an oak
I found the arrow, still unbroke;
And the song, from beginning to end,
I found again in the heart of a friend.

VOICES OF THE NIGHT :
A PSALM OF LIFE

by Henry Wadsworth Longfellow

Tell me not, in mournful numbers,
Life is but an empty dream! —
For the soul is dead that slumbers,
And things are not what they seem.

Life is real! Life is earnest!
And the grave is not its goal;
Dust thou art, to dust returnest,
Was not spoken of the soul.

Not enjoyment, and not sorrow,
Is our destined end or way;
But to act, that each to-morrow
Find us farther than to-day.

Art is long, and Time is fleeting,
And our hearts, though stout and brave,
Still, like muffled drums, are beating
Funeral marches to the grave.

In the world's broad field of battle,
In the bivouac of Life,
Be not like dumb, driven cattle!
Be a hero in the strife!

Trust no Future, howe'er pleasant!
Let the dead Past bury its dead!
Act, — act in the living Present!
Heart within, and God o'erhead!

Lives of great men all remind us
We can make our lives sublime,
And, departing, leave behind us
Footprints on the sands of time;

Footprints, that perhaps another,
Sailing o'er life's solemn main,
A forlorn and shipwrecked brother,
Seeing, shall take heart again.

Let us, then, be up and doing,
With a heart for any fate;
Still achieving, still pursuing,
Learn to labor and to wait.

THE FIRST SNOWFALL

by James Russell Lowell

The snow had begun in the gloaming,
   And busily all the night
Had been heaping field and highway
   With a silence deep and white.
Every pine and fir and hemlock
   Wore ermine too dear for an earl,
And the poorest twig on the elm-tree
   Was ridged inch deep with pearl.
From sheds new-roofed with Carrara
   Came Chanticleer's muffled crow,
The stiff rails softened to swan's-down,
   And still fluttered down the snow.
I stood and watched by the window
   The noiseless work of the sky,
And the sudden flurries of snow-birds,
   Like brown leaves whirling by.
I thought of a mound in sweet Auburn
   Where a little headstone stood;
How the flakes were folding it gently,
   As did robins the babes in the wood.
Up spoke our own little Mabel,
   Saying, "Father, who makes it snow?"
And I told of the good All-father
   Who cares for us here below.
Again I looked at the snow-fall,
   And thought of the leaden sky
That arched o'er our first great sorrow,

When that mound was heaped so high.
I remembered the gradual patience
   That fell from that cloud like snow,
Flake by flake, healing and hiding
   The scar that renewed our woe.
And again to the child I whispered,
   "The snow that husheth all,
Darling, the merciful Father
   Alone can make it fall"
Then, with eyes that saw not, I kissed her;
   And she, kissing back, could not know
That my kiss was given to her sister,
   Folded close under deepening snow.

HORATIUS

by Thomas Babbington Macaulay

A Lay Made About the Year Of The City CCCLX

I.
Lars Porsena of Closium
By the Nine Gods he swore
That the great house of Tarquin
Should suffer wrong no more.
By the Nine Gods he swore it,
And named a trysting day,
And bade his messengers ride forth,
East and west and south and north,
To summon his array.

II.
East and west and south and north
The messengers ride fast,
And tower and town and cottage
Have heard the trumpet's blast.
Shame on the false Etruscan
Who lingers in his home,
When Porsena of Clusium
Is on the march for Rome.

III.
The horsemen and the footmen
Are pouring in amain
From many a stately market-place,
From many a fruitful plain,
From many a lonely hamlet,

Which, hid by beech and pine,
Like an eagle's nest, hangs on the crest
Of purple Apennine;

IV.

From lordly Volaterræ¬Š Where scowls the far-famed hold
Piled by the hands of giants
For godlike kings of old;
From seagirt Populonia,
Whose sentinels descry
Sardinia's snowy mountain-tops
Fringing the southern sky;

V.

From the proud mart of Pisæ¬Š Queen of the western waves,
Where ride Massilia's triremes
Heavy with fair-haired slaves;
From where sweet Clanis wanders
Through corn and vines and flowers;
From where Cortona lifts to heaven
Her diadem of towers.

VI.

Tall are the oaks whose acorns
Drop in dark Auser's rill;
Fat are the stags that champ the boughs
Of the Ciminian hill;
Beyond all streams Clitumnus
Is to the herdsman dear;
Best of all pools the fowler loves
The great Volsinian mere.

VII.
But now no stroke of woodman
Is heard by Auser's rill;
No hunter tracks the stag's green path
Up the Ciminian hill;
Unwatched along Clitumnus
Grazes the milk-white steer;
Unharmed the water fowl may dip
In the Volsminian mere.

VIII.
The harvests of Arretium,
This year, old men shall reap;
This year, young boys in Umbro
Shall plunge the struggling sheep;
And in the vats of Luna,
This year, the must shall foam
Round the white feet of laughing girls
Whose sires have marched to Rome.

IX.
There be thirty chosen prophets,
The wisest of the land,
Who alway by Lars Porsena
Both morn and evening stand:
Evening and morn the Thirty
Have turned the verses o'er,
Traced from the right on linen white
By mighty seers of yore.

X.

And with one voice the Thirty
Have their glad answer given:
"Go forth, go forth, Lars Porsena;
Go forth, beloved of Heaven;
Go, and return in glory
To Clusium's royal dome;
And hang round Nurscia's altars
The golden shields of Rome."

XI.

And now hath every city
Sent up her tale of men;
The foot are fourscore thousand,
The horse are thousands ten.
Before the gates of Sutrium
Is met the great array.
A proud man was Lars Porsena
Upon the trysting day.

XII.

For all the Etruscan armies
Were ranged beneath his eye,
And many a banished Roman,
And many a stout ally;
And with a mighty following
To join the muster came
The Tusculan Mamilius,
Prince of the Latian name.

XIII.

But by the yellow Tiber
Was tumult and affright:
From all the spacious champaign
To Rome men took their flight.

A mile around the city,
The throng stopped up the ways;
A fearful sight it was to see
Through two long nights and days.

XIV.
For aged folks on crutches,
And women great with child,
And mothers sobbing over babes
That clung to them and smiled,
And sick men borne in litters
High on the necks of slaves,
And troops of sun-burned husbandmen
With reaping-hooks and staves,

XV.
And droves of mules and asses
Laden with skins of wine,
And endless flocks of goats and sheep,
And endless herds of kine,
And endless trains of wagons
That creaked beneath the weight
Of corn-sacks and of household goods,
Choked every roaring gate.

XVI.
Now, from the rock Tarpeian,
Could the wan burghers spy
The line of blazing villages
Red in the midnight sky.
The Fathers of the City,
They sat all night and day,
For every hour some horseman come
With tidings of dismay.

XVII.
To eastward and to westward
Have spread the Tuscan bands;
Nor house, nor fence, nor dovecote
In Crustumerium stands.
Verbenna down to Ostia
Hath wasted all the plain;
Astur hath stormed Janiculum,
And the stout guards are slain.

XVIII.
I wis, in all the Senate,[wis: know]
There was no heart so bold,
But sore it ached, and fast it beat,
When that ill news was told.
Forthwith up rose the Consul,
Up rose the Fathers all;
In haste they girded up their gowns,
And hied them to the wall.

XIX.
They held a council standing,
Before the River-Gate;
Short time was there, ye well may guess,
For musing or debate.
Out spake the Consul roundly:
"The bridge must straight go down;
For, since Janiculum is lost,
Nought else can save the town."

XX.

Just then a scout came flying,
All wild with haste and fear:
"To arms! to arms! Sir Consul:
Lars Porsena is here."
On the low hills to westward
The Consul fixed his eye,
And saw the swarthy storm of dust
Rise fast along the sky.

XXI.

And nearer fast and nearer
Doth the red whirlwind come;
And louder still and still more loud,
From underneath that rolling cloud,
Is heard the trumpet's war-note proud,
The trampling, and the hum.
And plainly and more plainly
Now through the gloom appears,
Far to left and far to right,
In broken gleams of dark-blue light,
The long array of helmets bright,
The long array of spears.

XXII.

And plainly and more plainly,
Above that glimmering line,
Now might ye see the banners
Of twelve fair cities shine;
But the banner of proud Clusium
Was highest of them all,
The terror of the Umbrian,
The terror of the Gaul.

XXIII.
And plainly and more plainly
Now might the burghers know,
By port and vest, by horse and crest,
Each warlike Lucumo.
There Cilnius of Arretium
On his fleet roan was seen;
And Astur of the four-fold shield,
Girt with the brand none else may
wield,
Tolumnius with the belt of gold,
And dark Verbenna from the hold
By reedy Thrasymene.

XXIV.
Fast by the royal standard,
O'erlooking all the war,
Lars Porsena of Clusium
Sat in his ivory car.
By the right wheel rode Mamilius,
Prince of the Latian name;
And by the left false Sextus,
That wrought the deed of shame.

XXV.
But when the face of Sextus
Was seen among the foes,
A yell that rent the firmament
From all the town arose.
On the house-tops was no woman
But spat towards him and hissed,
No child but screamed out curses,
And shook its little fist.

XXVI.

But the Consul's brow was sad,
And the Consul's speech was low,
And darkly looked he at the wall,
And darkly at the foe.
"Their van will be upon us
Before the bridge goes down;
And if they once may win the
bridge,
What hope to save the town?"

XXVII.

Then out spake brave Horatius,
The Captain of the Gate:
"To every man upon this earth
Death cometh soon or late.
And how can man die better
Than facing fearful odds,
For the ashes of his fathers,
And the temples of his gods,

XXVIII.

"And for the tender mother
Who dandled him to rest,
And for the wife who nurses
His baby at her breast,
And for the holy maidens
Who feed the eternal flame,
To save them from false Sextus
That wrought the deed of shame?

XXIX.

"Haul down the bridge, Sir Consul,
With all the speed ye may;
I, with two more to help me,
Will hold the foe in play.
In yon strait path a thousand

May well be stopped by three.
Now who will stand on either hand,
And keep the bridge with me?"

XXX.
Then out spake Spurius Lartius;
A Ramnian proud was he:
"Lo, I will stand at thy right hand,
And keep the bridge with thee."
And out spake strong Herminius;
Of Titian blood was he:
"I will abide on thy left side,
And keep the bridge with thee."

XXXI.
"Horatius," quoth the Consul,
"As thou sayest, so let it be."
And straight against that great array
Forth went the dauntless Three.
For Romans in Rome's quarrel
Spared neither land nor gold,
Nor son nor wife, nor limb nor life,
In the brave days of old.

XXXII.
Then none was for a party;
Then all were for the state;
Then the great man helped the poor,
And the poor man loved the great:
Then lands were fairly portioned;
Then spoils were fairly sold:
The Romans were like brothers
In the brave days of old.

XXXIII.
Now Roman is to Roman
More hateful than a foe,
And the Tribunes beard the high,
And the Fathers grind the low.
As we wax hot in faction,
In battle we wax cold:
Wherefore men fight not as they fought
In the brave days of old.

XXXIV.
Now while the Three were tightening
Their harness on their backs,
The Consul was the foremost man
To take in hand an axe:
And Fathers mixed with Commons
Seized hatchet, bar, and crow,
And smote upon the planks above,
And loosed the props below.

XXXV.
Meanwhile the Tuscan army,
Right glorious to behold,
Come flashing back the noonday light,
Rank behind rank, like surges bright
Of a broad sea of gold.
Four hundred trumpets sounded
A peal of warlike glee,
As that great host, with measured tread,
And spears advanced, and ensigns spread,
Rolled slowly towards the bridge's head,
Where stood the dauntless Three.

XXXVI.
The Three stood calm and silent,
And looked upon the foes,
And a great shout of laughter
From all the vanguard rose:
And forth three chiefs came spurring
Before that deep array;
To earth they sprang, their swords they drew,
And lifted high their shields, and flew
To win the narrrow way;

XXXVII.
Aunus from green Tifernum,
Lord of the Hill of Vines;
And Seius, whose eight hundred slaves
Sicken in Ilva's mines;
And Picus, long to Clusium
Vassal in peace and war,
Who led to fight his Umbrian powers
From that gray crag where, girt with towers,
The fortress of Nequinum lowers
O'er the pale waves of Nar.

XXXVIII.
Stout Lartius hurled down Aunus
Into the stream beneath;
Herminius struck at Seius,
And clove him to the teeth;
At Picus brave Horatius
Darted one fiery thrust;
And the proud Umbrian's gilded arms
Clashed in the bloody dust.

XXXIX.

Then Ocnus of Falerii
Rushed on the Roman Three;
And Lausulus of Urgo,
The rover of the sea;
And Aruns of Volsinium,
Who slew the great wild boar,
The great wild boar that had his den
Amidst the reeds of Cosa's fen,
And wasted fields, and slaughtered men,
Along Albinia's shore.

XL.

Herminius smote down Aruns:
Lartius laid Ocnus low:
Right to the heart of Lausulus
Horatius sent a blow.
"Lie there," he cried, "fell pirate!
No more, aghast and pale,
From Ostia's walls the crowd shall mark
The track of thy destroying bark.
No more Campania's hinds shall fly
To woods and caverns when they spy
Thy thrice accursed sail."

XLI.

But now no sound of laughter
Was heard among the foes.
A wild and wrathful clamor
From all the vanguard rose.
Six spears' lengths from the entrance
Halted that deep array,
And for a space no man came forth
To win the narrow way.

XLII.
But hark! the cry is Astur:
And lo! the ranks divide;
And the great Lord of Luna
Comes with his stately stride.
Upon his ample shoulders
Clangs loud the four-fold shield,
And in his hand he shakes the brand
Which none but he can wield.

XLIII.
He smiled on those bold Romans
A smile serene and high;
He eyed the flinching Tuscans,
And scorn was in his eye.
Quoth he, "The she-wolf's litter
Stand savagely at bay:
But will ye dare to follow,
If Astur clears the way?"

XLIV.
Then, whirling up his broadsword
With both hands to the height,
He rushed against Horatius,
And smote with all his might.
With shield and blade Horatius
Right deftly turned the blow.
The blow, though turned, came yet too nigh;
It missed his helm, but gashed his thigh:
The Tuscans raised a joyful cry
To see the red blood flow.

XLV.
He reeled, and on Herminius
He leaned one breathing-space;
Then, like a wild cat mad with wounds,
Sprang right at Astur's face.
Through teeth, and skull, and helmet
So fierce a thrust he sped,
The good sword stood a hand-breadth
out
Behind the Tuscan's head.

XLVI.
And the great Lord of Luna
Fell at that deadly stroke,
As falls on Mount Alvernus
A thunder smitten oak:
Far o'er the crashing forest
The giant arms lie spread;
And the pale augurs, muttering low,
Gaze on the blasted head.

XLVII.
On Astur's throat Horatius
Right firmly pressed his heel,
And thrice and four times tugged amain,
Ere he wrenched out the steel.
"And see," he cried, "the welcome,
Fair guests, that waits you here!
What noble Lucomo comes next
To taste our Roman cheer?"

XLVIII.
But at his haughty challange
A sullen murmur ran,
Mingled of wrath, and shame, and
dread,
Along that glittering van.
There lacked not men of prowess,
Nor men of lordly race;
For all Etruria's noblest
Were round the fatal place.

XLIX.
But all Etruria's noblest
Felt their hearts sink to see
On the earth the bloody corpses,
In the path the dauntless Three:
And, from the ghastly entrance
Where those bold Romans stood,
All shrank, like boys who unaware,
Ranging the woods to start a hare,
Come to the mouth of the dark lair
Where, growling low, a fierce old bear
Lies amidst bones and blood.

L.
Was none who would be foremost
To lead such dire attack;
But those behind cried, "Forward!"
And those before cried, "Back!"
And backward now and forward
Wavers the deep array;
And on the tossing sea of steel
To and frow the standards reel;
And the victorious trumpet-peal
Dies fitfully away.

LI.
Yet one man for one moment
Strode out before the crowd;
Well known was he to all the Three,
And they gave him greeting loud.
"Now welcome, welcome, Sextus!
Now welcome to thy home!
Why dost thou stay, and turn away?
Here lies the road to Rome."

LII.
Thrice looked he at the city;
Thrice looked he at the dead;
And thrice came on in fury,
And thrice turned back in dread:
And, white with fear and hatred,
Scowled at the narrow way
Where, wallowing in a pool of blood,
The bravest Tuscans lay.

LIII.
But meanwhile axe and lever
Have manfully been plied;
And now the bridge hangs tottering
Above the boiling tide.
"Come back, come back, Horatius!"
Loud cried the Fathers all.
"Back, Lartius! back, Herminius!
Back, ere the ruin fall!"

LIV.
Back darted Spurius Lartius;
Herminius darted back:
And, as they passed, beneath their feet
They felt the timbers crack.
But when they turned their faces,

And on the farther shore
Saw brave Horatius stand alone,
They would have crossed once more.

LV.
But with a crash like thunder
Fell every loosened beam,
And, like a dam, the mighty wreck
Lay right athwart the stream:
And a long shout of triumph
Rose from the walls of Rome,
As to the highest turret-tops
Was splashed the yellow foam.

LVI.
And, like a horse unbroken
When first he feels the rein,
The furious river struggled hard,
And tossed his tawny mane,
And burst the curb and bounded,
Rejoicing to be free,
And whirling down, in fierce career,
Battlement, and plank, and pier,
Rushed headlong to the sea.

LVII.
Alone stood brave Horatius,
But constant still in mind;
Thrice thirty thousand foes before,
And the broad flood behind.
"Down with him!" cried false Sextus,
With a smile on his pale face.
"Now yield thee," cried Lars Porsena,
"Now yield thee to our grace."

LVIII.
Round turned he, as not deigning
Those craven ranks to see;
Nought spake he to Lars Porsena,
To Sextus nought spake he;
But he saw on Palatinus
The white porch of his home;
And he spake to the noble river
That rolls by the towers of Rome.

LVIX.
"Oh, Tiber! Father Tiber!
To whom the Romans pray,
A Roman's life, a Roman's arms,
Take thou in charge this day!"
So he spake, and speaking sheathed
The good sword by his side,
And with his harness on his back,
Plunged headlong in the tide.

LX.
No sound of joy or sorrow
Was heard from either bank;
But friends and foes in dumb surprise,
With parted lips and straining eyes,
Stood gazing where he sank;
And when above the surges,
They saw his crest appear,
All Rome sent forth a rapturous cry,
And even the ranks of Tuscany
Could scarce forbear to cheer.

LXI.

But fiercely ran the current,
Swollen high by months of rain:
And fast his blood was flowing;
And he was sore in pain,
And heavy with his armor,
And spent with changing blows:
And oft they thought him sinking,
But still again he rose.

LXII.

Never, I ween, did swimmer,
In such an evil case,
Struggle through such a raging flood
Safe to the landing place:
But his limbs were borne up bravely
By the brave heart within,
And our good father Tiber
Bare bravely up his chin.

LXIII.

"Curse on him!" quoth false Sextus;
"Will not the villain drown?
But for this stay, ere close of day
We should have sacked the town!"
"Heaven help him!" quoth Lars Porsena
"And bring him safe to shore;
For such a gallant feat of arms
Was never seen before."

LXIV.

And now he feels the bottom;
Now on dry earth he stands;
Now round him throng the Fathers;
To press his gory hands;

And now, with shouts and clapping,
And noise of weeping loud,
He enters through the River-Gate
Borne by the joyous crowd.

LXV.
They gave him of the corn-land,
That was of public right,
As much as two strong oxen
Could plough from morn till night;
And they made a molten image,
And set it up on high,
And there is stands unto this day
To witness if I lie.

LXVI.
It stands in the Comitium
Plain for all folk to see;
Horatius in his harness,
Halting upon one knee:
And underneath is written,
In letters all of gold,
How valiantly he kept the bridge
In the brave days of old.

LXVII.
And still his name sounds stirring
Unto the men of Rome,
As the trumpet-blast that cries to them
To charge the Volscian home;
And wives still pray to Juno
For boys with hearts as bold
As his who kept the bridge so well
In the brave days of old.

LXVIII.
And in the nights of winter,
When the cold north winds blow,
And the long howling of the wolves
Is heard amidst the snow;
When round the lonely cottage
Roars loud the tempest's din,
And the good logs of Algidus
Roar louder yet within;

LXIX.
When the oldest cask is opened,
And the largest lamp is lit;
When the chestnuts glow in the embers,
And the kid turns on the spit;
When young and old in circle
Around the firebrands close;
When the girls are weaving baskets,
And the lads are shaping bows;

LXX.
When the goodman mends his armor,
And trims his helmet's plume;
When the goodwife's shuttle merrily
Goes flashing through the loom;
With weeping and with laughter
Still is the story told,
How well Horatius kept the bridge
In the brave days of old.

GOOD TIMBER

by Douglas Malloch

The tree that never had to fight
For sun and sky and air and light,
But stood out in the open plain
And always got its share of rain,
Never became a forest king
But lived and died a scrubby thing.
The man who never had to toil
To gain and farm his patch of soil,
Who never had to win his share
Of sun and sky and light and air,
Never became a manly man
But lived and died as he began.
Good timber does not grow with ease:
The stronger wind, the stronger trees;
The further sky, the greater length;
The more the storm, the more the strength.
By sun and cold, by rain and snow,
In trees and men good timbers grow.
Where thickest lies the forest growth,
We find the patriarchs of both.
And they hold counsel with the stars
Whose broken branches show the scars
Of many winds and much of strife.
This is the common law of life.

THE PASSIONATE SHEPHERD TO HIS LOVE

by Christopher Marlowe

Come live with me and be my love,
And we will all the pleasures prove,
That Valleys, groves, hills, and fields,
Woods, or steepy mountain yields.

And we will sit upon the Rocks,
Seeing the Shepherds feed their flocks,
By shallow Rivers to whose falls
Melodious birds sing Madrigals.

And I will make thee beds of Roses
And a thousand fragrant posies,
A cap of flowers, and a kirtle
Embroidered all with leaves of Myrtle;

A gown made of the finest wool
Which from our pretty Lambs we pull;
Fair lined slippers for the cold,
With buckles of the purest gold;

A belt of straw and Ivy buds,
With Coral clasps and Amber studs:
And if these pleasures may thee move,
Come live with me, and be my love.

The Shepherds' Swains shall dance and sing
For thy delight each May-morning:
If these delights thy mind may move,
Then live with me, and be my love.

SEA FEVER

by John Masefield

I must go down to the seas again, to the lonely sea and the sky,
And all I ask is a tall ship and a star to steer her by;
And the wheel's kick and the wind's song and the white sail's shaking,
And a grey mist on the sea's face, and a grey dawn breaking.

I must go down to the seas again, for the call of the running tide
Is a wild call and a clear call that may not be denied;
And all I ask is a windy day with the white clouds flying,
And the flung spray and the blown spume, and the sea-gulls crying.

I must go down to the seas again, to the vagrant gypsy life,
To the gull's way and the whale's way where the wind's like a whetted knife;
And all I ask is a merry yarn from a laughing fellow-rover,
And quiet sleep and a sweet dream when the long trick's over.

IN FLANDERS FIELDS

by Lieutenant-Colonel John McCrae

In Flanders fields the poppies blow
Between the crosses, row on row,
That mark our place; and in the sky
The larks, still bravely singing, fly
Scarce heard amid the guns below.

We are the Dead.
Short days ago
We lived, felt dawn, saw sunset glow,
Loved and were loved, and now we lie
In Flanders fields.

Take up our quarrel with the foe:
To you from failing hands we throw
The torch; be yours to hold it high.
If ye break faith with us who die
We shall not sleep, though poppies grow
In Flanders fields.

PARADISE LOST

by John Milton

OF Mans First Disobedience, and the Fruit
Of that Forbidden Tree, whose mortal tast
Brought Death into the World, and all our woe,
With loss of *Eden*, till one greater Man
Restore us, and regain the blissful Seat,
Sing Heav'nly Muse, that on the secret top
Of *Oreb*, or of *Sinai*, didst inspire
That Shepherd, who first taught the chosen Seed,
In the Beginning how the Heav'ns and Earth
Rose out of *Chaos*: or if *Sion* Hill
Delight thee more, and *Siloa's* brook that flow'd
Fast by the Oracle of God; I thence
Invoke thy aid to my adventrous Song,
That with no middle flight intends to soar
Above th' *Aonian* Mount, while it pursues
Things unattempted yet in Prose or Rhime.
And chiefly Thou, O Spirit, that dost prefer
Before all Temples th' upright heart and pure,
Instruct me, for Thou know'st; Thou from the first
Wast present, and with mighty wings outspread
Dove-like satst brooding on the vast Abyss
And mad'st it pregnant: What in me is dark
Illumin, what is low raise and support;
That to the highth of this great Argument
I may assert Eternal Providence,
And justifie the wayes of God to men.

Say first, for Heav'n hides nothing from thy view
Nor the deep Tract of Hell, say first what cause
Mov'd our Grand Parents in that happy State,
Favour'd of Heav'n so highly, to fall off
From thir Creator, and transgress his Will
For one restraint, Lords of the World besides?
Who first seduc'd them to that foul revolt?
Th' infernal Serpent; he it was, whose guile
Stird up with Envy and Revenge, deceiv'd
The Mother of Mankind, what time his Pride
Had cast him out from Heav'n, with all his Host
Of Rebel Angels, by whose aid aspiring
To set himself in Glory above his Peers,
He trusted to have equal'd the most High,
If he oppos'd; and with ambitious aim
Against the Throne and Monarchy of God
Rais'd impious War in Heav'n and Battel proud
With vain attempt.   Him the Almighty Power
Hurld headlong flaming from th' Ethereal Skie
With hideous ruine and combustion down
To bottomless perdition, there to dwell
In Adamantine Chains and penal Fire,
Who durst defie th' Omnipotent to Arms.
Nine times the Space that measures Day and Night
To mortal men, he with his horrid crew
Lay vanquisht, rowling in the fiery Gulfe
Confounded though immortal: But his doom
Reserv'd him to more wrath; for now the thought
Both of lost happiness and lasting pain
Torments him; round he throws his baleful eyes
That witness'd huge affliction and dismay
Mixt with obdurate pride and stedfast hate:
At once as far as Angels kenn he views
The dismal Situation waste and wilde,
A Dungeon horrible, on all sides round
As one great Furnace flam'd, yet from those flames

No light, but rather darkness visible
Serv'd onely to discover sights of woe,
Regions of sorrow, doleful shades, where peace
And rest can never dwell, hope never comes
That comes to all; but torture without end
Still urges, and a fiery Deluge, fed
With ever-burning Sulphur unconsum'd:
Such place Eternal Justice had prepar'd
For those rebellious, here thir prison ordained
In utter darkness, and thir portion set
As far remov'd from God and light of Heav'n
As from the Center thrice to th' utmost Pole.
O how unlike the place from whence they fell!
There the companions of his fall, o'rewhelm'd
With Floods and Whirlwinds of tempestuous fire,
He soon discerns, and weltring by his side
One next himself in power, and next in crime,
Long after known in *Palestine*, and nam'd
Beelzebub. To whom th' Arch-Enemy,
And thence in Heav'n call'd Satan, with bold words
Breaking the horrid silence thus began.

If thou beest he; But O how fall'n! how chang'd
From him, who in the happy Realms of Light
Cloth'd with transcendent brightness didst out-shine
Myriads though bright: If he whom mutual league,
United thoughts and counsels, equal hope
And hazard in the Glorious Enterprize,
Joynd with me once, now misery hath joynd
In equal ruin: into what Pit thou seest
From what highth fall'n, so much the stronger prov'd
He with his Thunder: and till then who knew
The force of those dire Arms?   yet not for those,
Nor what the Potent Victor in his rage
Can else inflict, do I repent or change,
Though chang'd in outward lustre; that fixt mind
And high disdain, from sence of injur'd merit,
That with the mightiest rais'd me to contend,

188

And to the fierce contention brought along
Innumerable force of Spirits arm'd
That durst dislike his reign, and me preferring,
His utmost power with adverse power oppos'd
In dubious Battel on the Plains of Heav'n,
And shook his throne.   What though the field be lost?
All is not lost; the unconquerable Will,
And study of revenge, immortal hate,
And courage never to submit or yield:
And what is else not to be overcome?
That Glory never shall his wrath or might
Extort from me.   To bow and sue for grace
With suppliant knee, and deifie his power,
Who from the terrour of this Arm so late
Doubted his Empire, that were low indeed,
That were an ignominy and shame beneath
This downfall; since by Fate the strength of Gods
And this Empyreal substance cannot fail,
Since through experience of this great event
In Arms not worse, in foresight much advanc't,
We may with more successful hope resolve
To wage by force or guile eternal Warr
Irreconcileable, to our grand Foe,
Who now triumphs, and in th' excess of joy
Sole reigning holds the Tyranny of Heav'n.

So spake th' Apostate Angel, though in pain,
Vaunting aloud, but rackt with deep despare:
And him thus answer'd soon his bold Compeer.

O Prince, O Chief of many Throned Powers,
That led th' imbattelld Seraphim to Warr
Under thy conduct, and in dreadful deeds
Fearless, endanger'd Heav'ns perpetual King;
And put to proof his high Supremacy,
Whether upheld by strength, or Chance, or Fate,
Too well I see and rue the dire event,
That with sad overthrow and foul defeat

Hath lost us Heav'n, and all this mighty Host
In horrible destruction laid thus low,
As far as Gods and Heav'nly Essences
Can perish: for the mind and spirit remains
Invincible, and vigour soon returns,
Though all our Glory extinct and happy state
Here swallow'd up in endless misery.
But what if he our Conquerour, (whom I now
Of force believe Almighty, since no less
Then such could hav orepow'rd such force as ours)
Have left us this our spirit and strength intire
Strongly to suffer and support our pains,
That we may so suffice his vengeful ire,
Or do him mightier service as his thralls
By right of Warr, what e're his business be
Here in the heart of Hell to work in Fire,
Or do his Errands in the gloomy Deep;
What can it then avail though yet we feel
Strength undiminisht, or eternal being
To undergo eternal punishment?
Whereto with speedy words th' Arch-fiend reply'd.

Fall'n Cherube, to be weak is miserable
Doing or Suffering: but of this be sure,
To do ought good never will be our task,
But ever to do ill our sole delight,
As being the contrary to his high will
Whom we resist.   If then his Providence
Out of our evil seek to bring forth good,
Our labour must be to pervert that end,
And out of good still to find means of evil;
Which oft times may succeed, so as perhaps
Shall grieve him, if I fail not, and disturb
His inmost counsels from thir destind aim.
But see the angry Victor hath recall'd
His Ministers of vengeance and pursuit
Back to the Gates of Heav'n: the Sulphurous Hail
Shot after us in storm, oreblown hath laid

The fiery Surge, that from the Precipice
Of Heav'n receiv'd us falling, and the Thunder,
Wing'd with red Lightning and impetuous rage,
Perhaps hath spent his shafts, and ceases now
To bellow through the vast and boundless Deep.
Let us not slip th' occasion, whether scorn,
Or satiate fury yield it from our Foe.
Seest thou yon dreary Plain, forlorn and wilde,
The seat of desolation, voyd of light,
Save what the glimmering of these livid flames
Casts pale and dreadful?   Thither let us tend
From off the tossing of these fiery waves,
There rest, if any rest can harbour there,
And reassembling our afflicted Powers,
Consult how we may henceforth most offend
Our Enemy, our own loss how repair,
How overcome this dire Calamity,
What reinforcement we may gain from Hope,
If not what resolution from despare.

Thus Satan to his neerest Mate
With Head up-lift above the wave, and Eyes
That sparkling blaz'd, his other Parts besides
Prone on the Flood, extended long and large
Lay floating many a rood, in bulk as huge
As whom the Fables name of monstrous size,
Titanian, or *Earth-born*, that warr'd on *Jove*,
Briareos or *Typhon*, whom the Den
By ancient *Tarsus* held, or that Sea-beast
Leviathan, which God of all his works
Created hugest that swim th' Ocean stream:
Him haply slumbring on the *Norway* foam
The Pilot of some small night-founder'd Skiff,
Deeming some Island, oft, as Sea-men tell,
With fixed Anchor in his skaly rind
Moors by his side under the Lee, while Night
Invests the Sea, and wished Morn delayes:
So stretcht out huge in length the Arch-fiend lay

Chain'd on the burning Lake, nor ever thence
Had ris'n or heav'd his head, but that the will
And high permission of all-ruling Heaven
Left him at large to his own dark designs,
That with reiterated crimes he might
Heap on himself damnation, while he sought
Evil to others, and enrag'd might see
How all his malice serv'd but to bring forth
Infinite goodness, grace and mercy shewn
On Man by him seduc't, but on himself
Treble confusion, wrath and vengeance pour'd.
Forthwith upright he rears from off the Pool
His mighty Stature; on each hand the flames
Drivn backward slope thir pointing spires, and rowld
In billows, leave i'th'midst a horrid Vale.
Then with expanded wings he stears his flight
Aloft, incumbent on the dusky Air
That felt unusual weight, till on dry Land
He lights, as if it were Land that ever burn'd
With solid, as the Lake with liquid fire;
And such appear'd in hue, as when the force
Of subterranean wind transports a Hill
Torn from *Pelorus*, or the shatter'd side
Of thundring *Aetna*, whose combustible
And fewel'd entrals thence conceiving Fire,
Sublim'd with Mineral fury, aid the Winds,
And leave a singed bottom all involv'd
With stench and smoak: Such resting found the sole
Of unblest feet.   Him followed his next Mate,
Both glorying to have scap't the *Stygian* flood
As Gods, and by thir own recover'd strength,
Not by the sufferance of supernal Power.

Is this the Region, this the Soil, the Clime,
Said then the lost Arch-Angel, this the seat
That we must change for Heav'n, this mournful gloom
For that celestial light?   Be it so, since he
Who now is Sovran can dispose and bid

What shall be right: fardest from him his best
Whom reason hath equald, force hath made supream
Above his equals.   Farewel happy Fields
Where Joy for ever dwells: Hail horrours, hail
Infernal world, and thou profoundest Hell
Receive thy new Possessor: One who brings
A mind not to be chang'd by Place or Time.
The mind is its own place, and in it self
Can make a Heav'n of Hell, a Hell of Heav'n.
What matter where, if I be still the same,
And what I should be, all but less then he
Whom Thunder hath made greater? Here at least
We shall be free; th' Almighty hath not built
Here for his envy, will not drive us hence:
Here we may reign secure, and in my choyce
To reign is worth ambition though in Hell:
Better to reign in Hell, then serve in Heav'n.
But wherefore let we then our faithful friends,
Th' associates and copartners of our loss
Lye thus astonisht on th' oblivious Pool,
And call them not to share with us their part
In this unhappy Mansion, or once more
With rallied Arms to try what may be yet
Regaind in Heav'n, or what more lost in Hell?

So *Satan* spake, and him *Beelzebub*
Thus answer'd.   Leader of those Armies bright,
Which but th' Omnipotent none could have foyld,
If once they hear that voyce, thir liveliest pledge
Of hope in fears and dangers, heard so oft
In worst extreams, and on the perilous edge
Of battel when it rag'd, in all assaults
Thir surest signal, they will soon resume
New courage and revive, though now they lye
Groveling and prostrate on yon Lake of Fire,
As we erewhile, astounded and amaz'd,
No wonder, fall'n such a pernicious highth.

He scarce had ceas't when the superiour Fiend
Was moving toward the shoar; his ponderous shield
Ethereal temper, massy, large and round,
Behind him cast; the broad circumference
Hung on his shoulders like the Moon, whose Orb
Through Optic Glass the *Tuscan* Artist views
At Ev'ning from the top of *Fesole*,
Or in *Valdarno*, to descry new Lands,
Rivers or Mountains in her spotty Globe.
His Spear, to equal which the tallest Pine
Hewn on *Norwegian* hills, to be the Mast
Of some great Ammiral, were but a wand,
He walkt with to support uneasie steps
Over the burning Marle, not like those steps
On Heavens Azure, and the torrid Clime
Smote on him sore besides, vaulted with Fire;
Nathless he so endur'd, till on the Beach
Of that inflamed Sea, he stood and call'd
His Legions, Angel Forms, who lay intrans't
Thick as Autumnal Leaves that strow the Brooks
In *Vallombrosa*, where th' *Etrurian* shades
High overarch't imbowr; or scatterd sedge
Afloat, when with fierce Winds *Orion* arm'd
Hath vext the Red-Sea Coast, whose waves orethrew
Busirus and his *Memphian* Chivalry,
While with perfidious hatred they pursu'd
The Sojourners of *Goshen*, who beheld
From the safe shore thir floating Carkases
And broken Chariot Wheels, so thick bestrown
Abject and lost lay these, covering the Flood,
Under amazement of thir hideous change.
He call'd so loud, that all the hollow Deep
Of Hell resounded. Princes, Potentates
Warriers, the Flowr of Heav'n, once yours, now lost,
If such astonishment as this can sieze
Eternal spirits; or have ye chos'n this place
After the toyl of Battel to repose
Your wearied vertue, for the ease you find

To slumber here, as in the Vales of Heav'n?
Or in this abject posture have ye sworn
To adore the Conquerour?   who now beholds
Cherube and Seraph rowling in the Flood
With scatter'd Arms and Ensigns, till anon
His swift pursuers from Heav'n Gates discern
Th' advantage, and descending tread us down
Thus drooping, or with linked Thunderbolts
Transfix us to the bottom of this Gulfe.
Awake, arise, or be for ever fall'n.

They heard, and were abasht, and up they sprung
Upon the wing, as when men wont to watch
On duty, sleeping found by whom they dread,
Rouse and bestir themselves ere well awake.
Nor did they not perceave the evil plight
In which they were, or the fierce pains not feel;
Yet to thir Generals Voyce they soon obeyd
Innumerable.   As when the potent Rod
Of *Amrams* Son in *Egypts* evill day
Wav'd round the Coast, up call'd a pitchy cloud
Of *Locusts*, warping on the Eastern Wind,
That ore the Realm of impious *Pharaoh* hung
Like Night, and darken'd all the Land of *Nile*:
So numberless were those bad Angels seen
Hovering on wing under the Cope of Hell
'Twixt upper, nether, and surrounding Fires;
Till, as a signal giv'n, th' uplifted Spear
Of thir great Sultan waving to direct
Thir course, in even ballance down they light
On the firm brimstone, and fill all the Plain;
A multitude, like which the populous North
Pour'd never from her frozen loyns, to pass
Rhene or the *Danaw*, when her barbarous Sons
Came like a Deluge on the South, and spread
Beneath *Gibralter* to the *Lybian* sands.
Forthwith from every Squadron and each Band
The Heads and Leaders thither hast where stood

Thir great Commander; Godlike shapes and forms
Excelling human, Princely Dignities,
And Powers that earst in Heaven sat on Thrones;
Though of thir Names in heav'nly Records now
Be no memorial blotted out and ras'd
By thir Rebellion, from the Books of Life.
Nor had they yet among the Sons of *Eve*
Got them new Names, till wandring ore the Earth,
Through Gods high sufferance for the tryal of man,
By falsities and lyes the greatest part
Of Mankind they corrupted to forsake
God thir Creator, and th' invisible
Glory of him that made them, to transform
Oft to the Image of a Brute, adorn'd
With gay Religions full of Pomp and Gold,
And Devils to adore for Deities:
Then were they known to men by various Names,
And various Idols through the Heathen World.
Say, Muse, the Names then known, who first, who last,
Rous'd from the slumber, on that fiery Couch,
At thir great Emperors call, as next in worth
Came singly where he stood on the bare strand,
While the promiscuous croud stood yet aloof?
The chief were those who from the Pit of Hell
Roaming to seek thir prey on earth, durst fix
Thir Seats long after next the Seat of God,
Thir Altars by his Altar, Gods ador'd
Among the Nations round, and durst abide
Jehovah thundring out of *Sion*, thron'd
Between the Cherubim; yea, often plac'd
Within his Sanctuary it self thir Shrines,
Abominations; and with cursed things
His holy Rites, and solemn Feasts profan'd,
And with thir darkness durst affront his light.
First *Moloch*, horrid King besmear'd with blood
Of human sacrifice, and parents tears,
Though for the noyse of Drums and Timbrels loud
Thir childrens cries unheard, that past through fire

To his grim Idol.   Him the *Ammonite*
Worshipt in *Rabba* and her watry Plain,
In *Argob* and in *Basan*, to the stream
Of utmost *Arnon*.   Not content with such
Audacious neighbourhood, the wisest heart
Of *Solomon* he led by fraud to build
His Temple right against the Temple of God
On that opprobrious Hill, and made his Grove
The pleasant Vally of *Hinnom*, *Tophet* thence
And black *Gehenna* call'd, the Type of Hell.
Next *Chemos*, th' obscene dread of *Moabs* Sons,
From *Aroar* to *Nebo*, and the wild
Of Southmost *Abarim*; in *Hesebon*
And *Heronaim*, *Seons* Realm, beyond
The flowry Dale of *Sibma* clad with Vines,
And *Eleale* to th' *Asphaltick* Pool.
Peor his other Name, when he entic'd
Israel in *Sittim* on thir march from *Nile*
To do him wanton rites, which cost them woe.
Yet thence his lustful Orgies he enlarg'd
Even to that Hill of scandal, but the Grove
Of *Moloch* homicide, lust hard by hate;
Till good *Josiah* drove them hence to Hell.
With these cam they, who from the bordring flood
Of old *Euphrates* to the Brook that parts
Egypt from *Syrian ground*, had general names
Of *Baalim* and *Ashtaroth*, those male,
These Feminine.   For Spirits when they please
Can either Sex assume, or both; so soft
And uncompounded is thir Essence pure,
Nor ti'd or manacl'd with joynt or limb,
Nor founded on the brittle strength of bones,
Like cumbrous flesh; but in what shape they choose
Dilated or condens't, bright or obscure,
Can execute thir aerie purposes,
And works of love or enmity fulfill.
For those the Race of *Israel* oft forsook
Thir living strength, and unfrequented left

His righteous Altar, bowing lowly down
To bestial Gods; for which thir heads as low
Bow'd down in Battel, sunk before the Spear
Of despicable foes.   With these in troop
Came *Astoreth*, whom the *Phoenicians* call'd
Astarte, Queen of Heav'n, with crescent Horns;
To whose bright Image nightly by the Moon
Sidonian Virgins paid thir Vows and Songs,
In *Sion* also not unsung, where stood
Her Temple on th' offensive Mountain, built
By that uxorious King, whose heart though large,
Beguil'd by fair Idolatresses, fell
To idols foul.   *Thammuz* came next behind,
Whose annual wound in *Lebanon* allur'd
The *Syrian* Damsels to lament his fate
In amorous dittyes all a Summers day,
While smooth *Adonis* from his native Rock
Ran purple to the Sea, suppos'd with blood
Of *Thammuz* yearly wounded; the Love-tale
Infected *Sions* daughters with like heat,
Whose wanton passions in the sacred Porch
Ezekial saw, when by the Vision led
His eye survay'd the dark Idolatries
Of alienated *Judah*.   Next came one
Who mourn'd in earnest, when the Captive Ark
Maim'd his brute Image, head and hands lopt off
In his own Temple, on the grunsel edge,
Where he fell flat, and sham'd his Worshipers:
Dagon his Name, Sea Monster, upward Man
And downward Fish: yet had his Temple high
Rear'd in *Azotus*, dreaded through the Coast
Of *Palestine*, in *Gath* and *Ascalon*
And *Accaron* and *Gaza's* frontier bounds.
Him follow'd *Rimmon*, whose delightful Seat
Was fair *Damascus*, on the fertil Banks
Of *Abbana* and *Pharphar*, lucid streams.
He also against the house of God was bold:
A Leper once he lost and gain'd a King,

Ahaz his sottish Conquerour, whom he drew
Gods Altar to disparage and displace
For one of *Syrian* mode, whereon to burn
His odious offrings, and adore the Gods
Whom he had vanquisht.   After these appear'd
A crew who under Names of old Renown,
Osiris, Isis, Orus and thir Train
With monstrous shapes and sorceries abus'd
Fanatic *Egypt* and her Priests, to seek
Thir wandring Gods Disguis'd in brutish forms
Rather then human.   Nor did *Israel* scape
Th' infection when thir borrow'd Gold compos'd
The Calf in *Oreb*: and the Rebel King
Doubl'd that sin in *Bethel* and in *Dan*,
Lik'ning his Maker to the Grazed Ox,
Jehovah, who in one Night when he pass'd
From *Egypt* marching, equal'd with one stroke
Both her first born and all her bleating Gods
Belial came last, then whom a Spirit more lewd
Fell not from Heaven, or more gross to love
Vice for it self: To him no Temple stood
Or Altar smoak'd; yet who more oft then hee
In Temples and at Altars, when the Priest
Turns Atheist, as did *Ely's* Sons, who fill'd
With lust and violence the house of God.
In Courts and Palaces he also Reigns
And in luxurious Cities, where the noyse
Of riot ascends above thir loftiest Towrs,
And injury and outrage: And when Night
Darkens the Streets, then wander forth the Sons
Of *Belial*, flown with insolence and wine.
Witness the Streets of *Sodom*, and that night
In *Gibeah*, when the hospitable door
Expos'd a Matron to avoid worse rape.
These were the prime in order and in might;
The rest were long to tell, though far renown'd,
Th' *Ionian* Gods, of *Javans* issue held
Gods, yet confest later then Heav'n and Earth

Thir boasted Parents; *Titan* Heav'ns first born
With his enormous brood, and birthright seis'd
By younger *Saturn*, he from mightier *Jove*
His own and *Rhea's* Son like measure found;
So *Jove* usurping reign'd: these first in *Creet*
And *Ida* known, thence on the Snowy top
Of cold *Olympus* rul'd the middle Air
Thir highest Heav'n; or on the *Delphian* Cliff,
Or in *Dodona*, and through all the bounds
Of *Doric* Land; or who with *Saturn* old
Fled over *Adria* to th' *Hesperian* Fields,
And ore the *Celtic* roam'd the utmost Isles.
All these and more came flocking; but with looks
Down cast and damp, yet such wherein appear'd
Obscure some glimps of joy, to have found thir chief
Not in despair, to have found themselves not lost
In loss itself; which on his count'nance cast
Like doubtful hue: but he his wonted pride
Soon recollecting, with high words, that bore
Semblance of worth, not substance, gently rais'd
Thir fanting courage, and dispel'd thir fears.
Then strait commands that at the warlike sound
Of Trumpets loud and Clarions be upreard
His mighty Standard; that proud honour claim'd
Azazel as his right, a Cherube tall:
Who forthwith from the glittering Staff unfurld
Th' Imperial Ensign, which full high advanc't
Shon like a Meteor streaming to the Wind
With Gemms and Golden lustre rich imblaz'd,
Seraphic arms and Trophies: all the while
Sonorous mettal blowing Martial sounds:
At which the universal Host upsent
A shout that tore Hells Concave, and beyond
Frighted the Reign of *Chaos* and old Night.
All in a moment through the gloom were seen
Ten thousand Banners rise into the Air
With Orient Colours waving: with them rose
A Forrest huge of Spears: and thronging Helms

Appear'd, and serried Shields in thick array
Of depth immeasurable: Anon they move
In perfect *Phalanx* to the *Dorian* mood
Of Flutes and soft Recorders; such as rais'd
To hight of noblest temper Hero's old
Arming to Battel, and in stead of rage
Deliberate valour breath'd, firm and unmov'd
With dread of death to flight or foul retreat,
Nor wanting power to mitigate and swage
With solemn touches, troubl'd thoughts, and chase
Anguish and doubt and fear and sorrow and pain
From mortal or immortal minds. Thus they
Breathing united force with fixed thought
Mov'd on in silence to soft Pipes that charm'd
Thir painful steps o're the burnt soyle; and now
Advanc't in view, they stand, a horrid Front
Of dreadful length and dazling Arms, in guise
Of Warriers old with order'd Spear and Shield,
Awaiting what command thir mighty Chief
Had to impose: He through the armed Files
Darts his experienc't eye, and soon traverse
The whole Battalion views, thir order due,
Thir visages and stature as of Gods,
Thir number last he summs. And now his heart
Distends with pride, and hardning in his strength
Glories: For never since created man,
Met such imbodied force, as nam'd with these
Could merit more then that small infantry
Warr'd on by Cranes: though all the Giant brood
Of *Phlegra* with th' Heroic Race were joyn'd
That fought at *Theb's* and *Ilium*, on each side
Mixt with auxiliar Gods; and what resounds
In Fable or *Romance* of *Uthers* Sons
Begirt with *British* and *Armoric* Knights;
And all who since Baptiz'd or Infidel
Jousted in *Aspramont* or *Montalban*,
Damasco, or *Marocco*, or *Trebisond*
Or whom *Biserta* sent from *Afric* shore

When *Charlemain* with all his Peerage fell
By *Fontarabbia*.   Thus far these beyond
Compare of mortal prowess, yet observ'd
Thir dread commander: he above the rest
In shape and gesture proudly eminent
Stood like a Towr; his form had yet not lost
All her Original brightness, nor appear'd
Less then Arch Angel ruind, and th' excess
Of Glory obscur'd;   As when the Sun new ris'n
Looks through the Horizontal misty Air
Shorn of his Beams, or from behind the Moon
In dim Eclips disastrous twilight sheds
On half the Nations, and with fear of change
Perplexes Monarch.   Dark'n'd so, yet shon
Above them all th' Arch Angel; but his face
Deep scars of Thunder had intrencht, and care
Sat on his faded cheek, but under Browes
Of dauntless courage, and considerate Pride
Waiting revenge: cruel his eye, but cast
Signs of remorse and passion to behold
The fellows of his crime, the followers rather
(Far other once beheld in bliss) condemn'd
For ever now to have thir lot in pain,
Millions of Spirits for his fault amerc't
Of Heav'n, and from Eternal Splendors flung
For his revolt, yet faithfull how they stood,
Thir Glory witherd.   As when Heavens Fire
Hath scath'd the Forrest Oaks, or Mountain Pines,
With singed top thir stately growth though bare
Stands on the blasted Heath.   He now prepar'd
To speak; whereat thir doubl'd Ranks they bend
From wing to wing, and half enclose him round
With all his Peers: attention held them mute.
Thrice he assayd, and thrice in spight of scorn,
Tears such as Angels weep, burst forth: at last
Words interwove with sighs found out thir way.

O Myriads of immortal Spirits, O Powers
Matchless, but with th' Almighty, and that strife
Was not inglorious, though th' event was dire,
As this place testifies, and this dire change
Hateful to utter: but what power of mind
Foreseeing or presaging, from the Depth
Of knowledge past or present, could have fear'd,
How such united force of Gods, how such
As stood like these, could ever know repulse?
For who can yet beleeve, though after loss,
That all these puissant Legions, whose exile
Hath emptied Heav'n, shall fail to re-ascend
Self-rais'd, and repossess thir native seat?
For mee be witness all the Host of Heav'n,
If counsels different, or danger shun'd
By mee, have lost our hopes.   But he who reigns
Monarch in Heav'n, till then as one secure
Sat on his Throne, upheld by old repute,
Consent or custome, and his Regal State
Put forth at full, but still his strength conceal'd,
Which tempted our attempt, and wrought our fall.
Henceforth his might we know, and know our own
So as not either to provoke, or dread
New warr, provok't; our better part remains
To work in close design, by fraud or guile
What force effected not: that he no less
At length from us may find, who overcomes
By force, hath overcome but half his foe.
Space may produce new Worlds; whereof so rife
There went a fame in Heav'n that he ere long
Intended to create, and therein plant
A generation, whom his choice regard
Should favour equal to the Sons of Heaven:
Thither, if but to pry, shall be perhaps
Our first eruption, thither or elsewhere:
For this Infernal Pit shall never hold
Caelestial Spirits in Bondage, nor th' Abyss
Long under darkness cover.   But these thoughts

Full Counsel must mature: Peace is despaird,
For who can think Submission? Warr then, Warr
Open or understood must be resolv'd.

He spake: and to confirm his words, out-flew
Millions of flaming swords, drawn from the thighs
Of mighty Cherubim; the sudden blaze
Far round illumin'd hell: highly they rag'd
Against the Highest, and fierce with grasped Arms
Clash'd on thir sounding Shields the din of war,
Hurling defiance toward the Vault of Heav'n.

There stood a hill not far whose griesly top
Belch'd fire and rowling smoak; the rest entire
Shon with a glossie scurff, undoubted sign
That in his womb was hid metallic Ore,
The work of Sulphur.   Thither wing'd with speed
A numerous Brigad hasten'd.   As when Bands
Of Pioners with Spade and Pickax arm'd
Forerun the Royal Camp, to trench a Field,
Or cast a Rampart.   *Mammon* led them on,
Mammon, the least erected Spirit that fell
From heav'n, for ev'n in heav'n his looks and thoughts
Were always downward bent, admiring more
The riches of Heav'ns pavement, trod'n Gold,
Then aught divine or holy else enjoy'd
In vision beatific: by him first
Men also, and by his suggestion taught
Ransack'd the Center, and with impious hands
Rifl'd the bowels of thir mother Earth
For Treasures better hid.   Soon had his crew
Op'nd into the Hill a spacious wound
And dig'd out ribs of Gold.   Let none admire
That riches grow in Hell; that soyle may best
Deserve the precious bane.   And here let those
Who boast in mortal things, and wond'ring tell
Of *Babel*, and the works of *Memphian* Kings
Learn how thir greatest Monuments of Fame,

And Strength and Art are easily out-done
By Spirits reprobate, and in an hour
What in an age they with incessant toyle
And hands innumerable scarce perform.
Nigh on the Plain in many cells prepar'd
That underneath had veins of liquid fire
Sluc'd from the Lake, a second multitude
With wond'rous Art found out the massie Ore,
Severing each kind, and scum'd the Bullion dross:
A third as soon had form'd within the ground
A various mould, and from the boyling cells
By strange conveyance fill'd each hollow nook,
As in an Organ from one blast of wind
To many a row of Pipes the sound-board breaths.
Anon out of the earth a Fabrick huge
Rose like an Exhalation, with the sound
Of Dulcet Symphonies and voices sweet,
Built like a Temple, where *Pilasters* round
Were set, and Doric pillars overlaid
With Golden Architrave; nor did there want
Cornice or Freeze, with bossy Sculptures grav'n,
The Roof was fretted Gold.   Not *Babilon*,
Nor great *Alcairo* such magnificence
Equal'd in all thir glories, to inshrine
Belus or *Serapis* thir Gods, or seat
Thir Kings, when *Aegypt* with *Assyria* strove
In wealth and luxurie.   Th' ascending pile
Stood fixt her stately highth, and strait the dores
Op'ning thir brazen foulds discover wide
Within, her ample spaces, o're the smooth
And level pavement: from the arched roof
Pendant by suttle Magic many a row
Of Starry Lamps and blazing Cressets fed
With *Naphtha* and *Asphaltus* yeilded light
As from a sky.   The hasty multitude
Admiring enter'd, and the work some praise
And some the Architect: his hand was known
In Heav'n by many a Towred structure high,

Where Scepter'd Angels held thir residence,
And sat as Princes, whom the supreme King
Exalted to such power, and gave to rule,
Each in his Hierarchie, the Orders bright.
Nor was his name unheard or unador'd
In ancient *Greece*; and in *Ausonian* land
Men call'd him *Mulciber*; and how he fell
From Heav'n, they fabl'd, thrown by angry *Jove*
Sheer o're the Chrystal Battlements; from Morn
To Noon he fell, from Noon to dewy Eve,
A Summers day; and with the setting Sun
Dropt from the Zenith like a falling Star,
On *Lemnos* th' *Aegaean* Ile: thus they relate,
Erring; for he with this rebellious rout
Fell long before; nor aught avail'd him now
To have built in Heav'n high Towrs; nor did he scape
By all his Engins, but was headlong sent
With his industrious crew to build in hell.
Mean while the winged Haralds by command
Of Sovran power, with awful Ceremony
And Trumpets sound throughout the Host proclaim
A solemn Councel forthwith to be held
At *Pandaemonium*, the high Capital
Of Satan and his Peers: thir summons call'd
From every Band and squared Regiment
By place or choice the worthiest; they anon
With hunderds and with thousands trooping came
Attended: all access was throng'd, the Gates
And Porches wide, but chief the spacious Hall
(Though like a cover'd field, where Champions bold
Wont ride in arm'd, and at the Soldans chair
Defi'd the best of *Panim* chivalry
To mortal combat or carreer with Lance)
Thick swarm'd, both on the ground and in the air,
Brusht with the hiss of russling wings.   As Bees
In spring time, when the Sun with *Taurus* rides,
Pour forth thir populous youth about the Hive
In clusters; they among fresh dews and flowers

Flie to and fro, or on the smoothed Plank,
The suburb of thir Straw-built Cittadel,
New rub'd with Baum, expatiate and confer
Thir State affairs.   So thick the aerie crowd
Swarm'd and were straitn'd; till the Signal giv'n
Behold a wonder! they but now who seemd
In bigness to surpass Earths Giant Sons
Now less then smallest Dwarfs, in narrow room
Throng numberless, like that Pigmean Race
Beyond the *Indian* Mount, or Faerie Elves,
Whose midnight Revels, by a Forrest side
Or Fountain some belated Peasant sees,
Or dreams he sees, while over-head the Moon
Sits Arbitress, and neerer to the Earth
Wheels her pale course, they on thir mirth and dance
Intent, with jocond Music charm his ear;
At once with joy and fear his heart rebounds.
Thus incorporeal Spirits to smallest forms
Reduc'd thir shapes immense, and were at large,
Though without number still amidst the Hall
Of that infernal Court.   But far within
And in thir own dimensions like themselves
The great Seraphic Lords and Cherubim
In close recess and secret conclave sat
A thousand Demy-Gods on golden seat's,
Frequent and full.   After short silence then
And summons read, the great consult began.

SONNET XIX:
WHEN I CONSIDER HOW MY LIGHT IS SPENT

by John Milton

When I consider how my light is spent,
    Ere half my days in this dark world and wide,
    And that one talent which is death to hide
Lodged with me useless, though my soul more bent
To serve therewith my Maker, and present
    My true account, lest He returning chide;
    "Doth God exact day-labor, light denied?"
I fondly ask. But Patience, to prevent
That murmur, soon replies, "God doth not need
    Either man's work or His own gifts. Who best
    Bear His mild yoke, they serve Him best. His state
Is kingly: thousands at His bidding speed,
    And post o'er land and ocean without rest;
    They also serve who only stand and wait."

POETRY

by Marianne Moore

I too, dislike it: there are things that are important beyond
    all this fiddle.
    Reading it, however, with a perfect contempt for it, one
       discovers that there is in
  it after all, a place for the genuine.
     Hands that can grasp, eyes
      that can dilate, hair that can rise
        if it must, these things are important not because a

high-sounding interpretation can be put upon them but because
    they are
  useful; when they become so derivative as to become
    unintelligible, the
  same thing may be said for all of us—that we
    do not admire what
    we cannot understand. The bat,
      holding on upside down or in quest of something to

eat, elephants pushing, a wild horse taking a roll, a tireless
    wolf under
  a tree, the immovable critic twinkling his skin like a horse
    that feels a flea, the base-
  ball fan, the statistician—case after case
    could be cited did
    one wish it; nor is it valid
      to discriminate against "business documents and

school-books"; all these phenomena are important. One must
    make a distinction
  however: when dragged into prominence by half poets,
    the result is not poetry,
 nor till the autocrats among us can be
   "literalists of
   the imagination"—above
    insolence and triviality and can present

for inspection, imaginary gardens with real toads in them,
    shall we have
  it. In the meantime, if you demand on the one hand, in defiance of their opinion—
  the raw material of poetry in
   all its rawness, and
   that which is on the other hand,
    genuine, then you are interested in poetry.

THE FISH

by Marianne Moore

wade
through black jade.
    Of the crow-blue mussel-shells, one keeps
    adjusting the ash-heaps;
        opening and shutting itself like

an
injured fan.
    The barnacles which encrust the side
    of the wave, cannot hide
        there for the submerged shafts of the

sun,
split like spun
    glass, move themselves with spotlight swiftness
    into the crevices—
        in and out, illuminating

the
turquoise sea
    of bodies. The water drives a wedge
    of iron through the iron edge
        of the cliff; whereupon the stars,

pink
rice-grains, ink-
    bespattered jelly fish, crabs like green
    lilies, and submarine
        toadstools, slide each on the other.

All
external
        marks of abuse are present on this
        defiant edifice—
                all the physical features of

ac-
cident—lack
        of cornice, dynamite grooves, burns, and
        hatchet strokes, these things stand
                out on it; the chasm-side is

dead.
Repeated
        evidence has proved that it can live
        on what can not revive
                its youth. The sea grows old in it.

I LIKE FOR YOU TO BE STILL

by Pablo Neruda

I like for you to be still
It is as though you are absent
And you hear me from far away
And my voice does not touch you
It seems as though your eyes had flown away
And it seems that a kiss had sealed your mouth
As all things are filled with my soul
You emerge from the things
Filled with my soul
You are like my soul
A butterfly of dream
And you are like the word: Melancholy

I like for you to be still
And you seem far away
It sounds as though you are lamenting
A butterfly cooing like a dove
And you hear me from far away
And my voice does not reach you
Let me come to be still in your silence
And let me talk to you with your silence
That is bright as a lamp
Simple, as a ring
You are like the night
With its stillness and constellations
Your silence is that of a star
As remote and candid

I like for you to be still
It is as though you are absent
Distant and full of sorrow
So you would've died
One word then, One smile is enough
And I'm happy;
Happy that it's not true

HERE I LOVE YOU

by Pablo Neruda

Here I love you.
In the dark pines the wind disentangles itself.
The moon glows like phosphorous on the vagrant waters.
Days, all one kind, go chasing each other.

The snow unfurls in dancing figures.
A silver gull slips down from the west.
Sometimes a sail. High, high stars.
Oh the black cross of a ship.
Alone.

Sometimes I get up early and even my soul is wet.
Far away the sea sounds and resounds.
This is a port.

Here I love you.
Here I love you and the horizon hides you in vain.
I love you still among these cold things.
Sometimes my kisses go on those heavy vessels
that cross the sea towards no arrival.
I see myself forgotten like those old anchors.

The piers sadden when the afternoon moors there.
My life grows tired, hungry to no purpose.
I love what I do not have. You are so far.
My loathing wrestles with the slow twilights.
But night comes and starts to sing to me.

The moon turns its clockwork dream.
The biggest stars look at me with your eyes.
And as I love you, the pines in the wind
want to sing your name with their leaves of wire.

TONIGHT I CAN WRITE (THE SADDEST LINES)

by Pablo Neruda

Tonight I can write the saddest lines.

Write, for example,
'The night is starry and the stars are blue and shiver in the distance.'

The night wind revolves in the sky and sings.

Tonight I can write the saddest lines.
I loved her, and sometimes she loved me too.

Through nights like this one I held her in my arms.
I kissed her again and again under the endless sky.

She loved me, sometimes I loved her too.
How could one not have loved her great still eyes.

Tonight I can write the saddest lines.
To think that I do not have her. To feel that I have lost her.

To hear the immense night, still more immense without her.
And the verse falls to the soul like dew to the pasture.

What does it matter that my love could not keep her.
The night is starry and she is not with me.

This is all. In the distance someone is singing. In the distance.
My soul is not satisfied that it has lost her.

My sight tries to find her as though to bring her closer.
My heart looks for her, and she is not with me.

The same night whitening the same trees.
We, of that time, are no longer the same.

I no longer love her, that's certain, but how I loved her.
My voice tried to find the wind to touch her hearing.

Another's. She will be another's. As she was before my kisses.
Her voice, her bright body. Her infinite eyes.

I no longer love her, that's certain, but maybe I love her.
Love is so short, forgetting is so long.

Because through nights like this one I held her in my arms
my soul is not satisfied that it has lost her.

Though this be the last pain that she makes me suffer
and these the last verses that I write for her.

ANNABEL LEE

by Edgar Allan Poe

It was many and many a year ago,
   In a kingdom by the sea,
That a maiden there lived whom you may know
   By the name of Annabel Lee;
And this maiden she lived with no other thought
   Than to love and be loved by me.
I was a child and she was a child,
   In this kingdom by the sea,
But we loved with a love that was more than love—
   I and my Annabel Lee—
With a love that the wingèd seraphs of Heaven
   Coveted her and me.
And this was the reason that, long ago,
   In this kingdom by the sea,
A wind blew out of a cloud, chilling
   My beautiful Annabel Lee;
So that her highborn kinsmen came
   And bore her away from me,
To shut her up in a sepulchre
   In this kingdom by the sea.
The angels, not half so happy in Heaven,
   Went envying her and me—
Yes!—that was the reason (as all men know,
   In this kingdom by the sea)
That the wind came out of the cloud by night,
   Chilling and killing my Annabel Lee.

But our love it was stronger by far than the love
    Of those who were older than we—
Of many far wiser than we—
    And neither the angels in Heaven above
Nor the demons down under the sea
    Can ever dissever my soul from the soul
Of the beautiful Annabel Lee;
For the moon never beams, without bringing me dreams
    Of the beautiful Annabel Lee;
And the stars never rise, but I feel the bright eyes
    Of the beautiful Annabel Lee;
 And so, all the night-tide, I lie down by the side
        Of my darling—my darling—my life and my bride,
        In her sepulchre there by the sea—
        In her tomb by the sounding sea.

A DREAM WITHIN A DREAM

by Edgar Allan Poe

Take this kiss upon the brow!
And, in parting from you now,
Thus much let me avow —
You are not wrong, who deem
That my days have been a dream;
Yet if hope has flown away
In a night, or in a day,
In a vision, or in none,
Is it therefore the less *gone*?
All that we see or seem
Is but a dream within a dream.

I stand amid the roar
Of a surf-tormented shore,
And I hold within my hand
Grains of the golden sand —
How few! yet how they creep
Through my fingers to the deep,
While I weep — while I weep!
O God! Can I not grasp
Them with a tighter clasp?
O God! can I not save
One from the pitiless wave?
Is *all* that we see or seem
But a dream within a dream?

ALONE

by Edgar Allan Poe

From childhood's hour I have not been
As others were—I have not seen
As others saw—I could not bring
My passions from a common spring—
From the same source I have not taken
My sorrow—I could not awaken
My heart to joy at the same tone—
And all I lov'd—I lov'd alone—
Then—in my childhood—in the dawn
Of a most stormy life—was drawn
From ev'ry depth of good and ill
The mystery which binds me still—
From the torrent, or the fountain—
From the red cliff of the mountain—
From the sun that 'round me roll'd
In its autumn tint of gold—
From the lightning in the sky
As it pass'd me flying by—
From the thunder, and the storm—
And the cloud that took the form
(When the rest of Heaven was blue)
Of a demon in my view—

THE RAVEN

by Edgar Allan Poe

Once upon a midnight dreary, while I pondered, weak and weary,
Over many a quaint and curious volume of forgotten lore—
While I nodded, nearly napping, suddenly there came a tapping,
As of some one gently rapping, rapping at my chamber door—
"'Tis some visitor," I muttered, "tapping at my chamber door—
      Only this and nothing more."
Ah, distinctly I remember it was in the bleak December;
And each separate dying ember wrought its ghost upon the floor.
Eagerly I wished the morrow;—vainly I had sought to borrow
From my books surcease of sorrow—sorrow for the lost Lenore—
For the rare and radiant maiden whom the angels name Lenore—
      Nameless here for evermore.
And the silken, sad, uncertain rustling of each purple curtain
Thrilled me—filled me with fantastic terrors never felt before;
So that now, to still the beating of my heart, I stood repeating,
"'Tis some visitor entreating entrance at my chamber door—
Some late visitor entreating entrance at my chamber door;—
      This it is and nothing more."
Presently my soul grew stronger; hesitating then no longer,
"Sir," said I, "or Madam, truly your forgiveness I implore;
But the fact is I was napping, and so gently you came rapping,
And so faintly you came tapping, tapping at my chamber door,
That I scarce was sure I heard you"—here I opened wide the door;—
      Darkness there and nothing more.
Deep into that darkness peering, long I stood there wondering, fearing,
Doubting, dreaming dreams no mortal ever dared to dream before;
But the silence was unbroken, and the stillness gave no token,

And the only word there spoken was the whispered word, "Lenore?"
This I whispered, and an echo murmured back the word, "Lenore!"—
      Merely this and nothing more.
Back into the chamber turning, all my soul within me burning,
Soon again I heard a tapping somewhat louder than before.
"Surely," said I, "surely that is something at my window lattice;
Let me see, then, what thereat is, and this mystery explore—
Let my heart be still a moment and this mystery explore;—
      'Tis the wind and nothing more!"
Open here I flung the shutter, when, with many a flirt and flutter,
In there stepped a stately Raven of the saintly days of yore;
Not the least obeisance made he; not a minute stopped or stayed he;
But, with mien of lord or lady, perched above my chamber door—
Perched upon a bust of Pallas just above my chamber door—
      Perched, and sat, and nothing more.
Then this ebony bird beguiling my sad fancy into smiling,
By the grave and stern decorum of the countenance it wore,
"Though thy crest be shorn and shaven, thou," I said, "art sure no craven,
Ghastly grim and ancient Raven wandering from the Nightly shore—
Tell me what thy lordly name is on the Night's Plutonian shore!"
      Quoth the Raven "Nevermore."
Much I marvelled this ungainly fowl to hear discourse so plainly,
Though its answer little meaning—little relevancy bore;
For we cannot help agreeing that no living human being
Ever yet was blest with seeing bird above his chamber door—
Bird or beast upon the sculptured bust above his chamber door,
      With such name as "Nevermore."
But the Raven, sitting lonely on the placid bust, spoke only
That one word, as if his soul in that one word he did outpour.
Nothing further then he uttered—not a feather then he fluttered—
Till I scarcely more than muttered "Other friends have flown before—
On the morrow he will leave me, as my hopes have flown before."
      Then the bird said "Nevermore."

Startled at the stillness broken by reply so aptly spoken,
"Doubtless," said I, "what it utters is its only stock and store
Caught from some unhappy master whom unmerciful Disaster
Followed fast and followed faster till his songs one burden bore—
Till the dirges of his Hope that melancholy burden bore
   Of 'Never—nevermore.'"

But the Raven still beguiling my sad fancy into smiling,
Straight I wheeled a cushioned seat in front of bird, and bust and door;
Then, upon the velvet sinking, I betook myself to linking
Fancy unto fancy, thinking what this ominous bird of yore—
What this grim, ungainly, ghastly, gaunt and ominous bird of yore
   Meant in croaking "Nevermore."

This I sat engaged in guessing, but no syllable expressing
To the fowl whose fiery eyes now burned into my bosom's core;
This and more I sat divining, with my head at ease reclining
On the cushion's velvet lining that the lamp-light gloated o'er,
But whose velvet violet lining with the lamp-light gloating o'er,
   She shall press, ah, nevermore!

Then, methought, the air grew denser, perfumed from an unseen censer
Swung by Seraphim whose foot-falls tinkled on the tufted floor.
"Wretch," I cried, "thy God hath lent thee—by these angels he hath sent thee
Respite—respite and nepenthe, from thy memories of Lenore;
Quaff, oh quaff this kind nepenthe and forget this lost Lenore!"
   Quoth the Raven "Nevermore."

"Prophet!" said I, "thing of evil!—prophet still, if bird or devil!—
Whether Tempter sent, or whether tempest tossed thee here ashore,
Desolate yet all undaunted, on this desert land enchanted—
On this home by Horror haunted—tell me truly, I implore—
Is there—is there balm in Gilead?—tell me—tell me, I implore!"
   Quoth the Raven "Nevermore."

"Prophet!" said I, "thing of evil—prophet still, if bird or devil!
By that Heaven that bends above us—by that God we both adore—
Tell this soul with sorrow laden if, within the distant Aidenn,
It shall clasp a sainted maiden whom the angels name Lenore—
Clasp a rare and radiant maiden whom the angels name Lenore."
   Quoth the Raven "Nevermore."

"Be that word our sign in parting, bird or fiend!" I shrieked,
upstarting—
"Get thee back into the tempest and the Night's Plutonian shore!
Leave no black plume as a token of that lie thy soul hath spoken!
Leave my loneliness unbroken!—quit the bust above my door!
Take thy beak from out my heart, and take thy form from off my door!"
       Quoth the Raven "Nevermore."
And the Raven, never flitting, still is sitting, still is sitting
On the pallid bust of Pallas just above my chamber door;
And his eyes have all the seeming of a demon's that is dreaming,
And the lamp-light o'er him streaming throws his shadow on the floor;
And my soul from out that shadow that lies floating on the floor
       Shall be lifted—nevermore!

ODE ON SOLITUDE

by Alexander Pope

Happy the man, whose wish and care
A few paternal acres bound,
Content to breathe his native air,
             In his own ground.

Whose heards with milk, whose fields with bread,
Whose flocks supply him with attire,
Whose trees in summer yield him shade,
             In winter fire.

Blest! who can unconcern'dly find
Hours, days, and years slide soft away,
In health of body, peace of mind,
             Quiet by day,

Sound sleep by night; study and ease
Together mix'd; sweet recreation,
And innocence, which most does please,
             With meditation.

Thus let me live, unseen, unknown;
Thus unlamented let me die;
Steal from the world, and not a stone
             Tell where I lye.

REMEMBER

by Christina Rossetti

Remember me when I am gone away,
　　Gone far away into the silent land;
　　When you can no more hold me by the hand,
Nor I half turn to go yet turning stay.
Remember me when no more day by day
　　You tell me of our future that you plann'd:
　　Only remember me; you understand
It will be late to counsel then or pray.
Yet if you should forget me for a while
　　And afterwards remember, do not grieve:
　　For if the darkness and corruption leave
　　A vestige of the thoughts that once I had,
Better by far you should forget and smile
　　Than that you should remember and be sad.

FOG

by Carl Sandburg

The fog comes
on little cat feet.

It sits looking
over harbor and city
on silent haunches
and then moves on.

DEATH IS NOTHING AT ALL

by *Henry Scott-Holland*

Death is nothing at all.
I have only slipped away to the next room.
I am I and you are you.
Whatever we were to each other,
That, we still are.

Call me by my old familiar name.
Speak to me in the easy way
which you always used.
Put no difference into your tone.
Wear no forced air of solemnity or sorrow.

Laugh as we always laughed
at the little jokes we enjoyed together.
Play, smile, think of me. Pray for me.
Let my name be ever the household word
that it always was.
Let it be spoken without effect.
Without the trace of a shadow on it.

Life means all that it ever meant.
It is the same that it ever was.
There is absolute unbroken continuity.
Why should I be out of mind
because I am out of sight?

I am but waiting for you.
For an interval.
Somewhere. Very near.
Just around the corner.

All is well.

I HAVE A RENDEZVOUS WITH DEATH

by Alan Seeger

I have a rendezvous with Death
At some disputed barricade
When Spring comes back with rustling shade
And apple blossoms fill the air.
I have a rendezvous with Death
When Spring brings back blue days and fair

It may be he shall take my hand
And lead me into his dark land
And close my eyes and quench my breath;
It may be I shall pass him, still,
I have a rendezvous with Death
On some scarred slope of battered hill,
When Spring comes round again this year
And the first meadow flowers appear.

God knows 'twere better to be deep
Pillowed in silk and scented down,
Where love throbs out in blissful sleep
Pulse nigh to pulse and breath to breath,
Where hushed awakenings are dear.
But I've a rendezvous with Death
At midnight in some flaming town,
When Spring trips north again this year,
And I to my pledged word am true.
I shall not fail that rendezvous.

A GRAIN OF SAND

by Robert W. Service

If starry space no limit knows
    And sun succeeds to sun,
There is no reason to suppose
    Our earth the only one.
'Mid countless constellations cast
    A million worlds may be,
With each a God to bless or blast
    And steer to destiny.

Just think! A million gods or so
    To guide each vital stream,
With over all to boss the show
    A Deity supreme.
Such magnitudes oppress my mind;
    From cosmic space it swings;
So ultimately glad to find
    Relief in little things.

For look! Within my hollow hand,
    While round the earth careens,
I hold a single grain of sand
    And wonder what it means.
Ah! If I had the eyes to see,
    And brain to understand,
I think Life's mystery might be
    Solved in this grain of sand.

233

THE CREMATION OF SAM MCGEE
by Robert W. Service

There are strange things done in the midnight sun
 By the men who moil for gold;
The Arctic trails have their secret tales
 That would make your blood run cold;
The Northern Lights have seen queer sights,
 But the queerest they ever did see
Was that night on the marge of Lake Lebarge
 I cremated Sam McGee.

Now Sam McGee was from Tennessee, where the cotton blooms and blows.
Why he left his home in the South to roam 'round the Pole, God only knows.
He was always cold, but the land of gold seemed to hold him like a spell;
Though he'd often say in his homely way that "he'd sooner live in hell."

On a Christmas Day we were mushing our way over the Dawson trail.
Talk of your cold! through the parka's fold it stabbed like a driven nail.
If our eyes we'd close, then the lashes froze till sometimes we couldn't see;
It wasn't much fun, but the only one to whimper was Sam McGee.

And that very night, as we lay packed tight in our robes beneath the snow,
And the dogs were fed, and the stars o'erhead were dancing heel and toe,
He turned to me, and "Cap," says he, "I'll cash in this trip, I guess;
And if I do, I'm asking that you won't refuse my last request."

Well, he seemed so low that I couldn't say no; then he says with a sort of moan:
"It's the cursèd cold, and it's got right hold till I'm chilled clean through to the bone.
Yet 'tain't being dead—it's my awful dread of the icy grave that pains;
So I want you to swear that, foul or fair, you'll cremate my last remains."

A pal's last need is a thing to heed, so I swore I would not fail;
And we started on at the streak of dawn; but God! he looked ghastly pale.
He crouched on the sleigh, and he raved all day of his home in Tennessee;
And before nightfall a corpse was all that was left of Sam McGee.

There wasn't a breath in that land of death, and I hurried, horror-driven,
With a corpse half hid that I couldn't get rid, because of a promise given;
It was lashed to the sleigh, and it seemed to say: "You may tax your brawn and brains,
But you promised true, and it's up to you to cremate those last remains."

Now a promise made is a debt unpaid, and the trail has its own stern code.
In the days to come, though my lips were dumb, in my heart how I cursed that load.
In the long, long night, by the lone firelight, while the huskies, round in a ring,
Howled out their woes to the homeless snows— O God! how I loathed the thing.

And every day that quiet clay seemed to heavy and heavier grow;
And on I went, though the dogs were spent and the grub was getting low;
The trail was bad, and I felt half mad, but I swore I would not give in;
And I'd often sing to the hateful thing, and it hearkened with a grin.

Till I came to the marge of Lake Lebarge, and a derelict there lay;
It was jammed in the ice, but I saw in a trice it was called the "Alice May."
And I looked at it, and I thought a bit, and I looked at my frozen chum;
Then "Here," said I, with a sudden cry, "is my cre-ma-tor-eum."

Some planks I tore from the cabin floor, and I lit the boiler fire;
Some coal I found that was lying around, and I heaped the fuel higher;
The flames just soared, and the furnace roared—such a blaze you seldom see;
And I burrowed a hole in the glowing coal, and I stuffed in Sam McGee.

Then I made a hike, for I didn't like to hear him sizzle so;
And the heavens scowled, and the huskies howled, and the wind began to blow.
It was icy cold, but the hot sweat rolled down my cheeks, and I don't know why;
And the greasy smoke in an inky cloak went streaking down the sky.

I do not know how long in the snow I wrestled with grisly fear;
But the stars came out and they danced about ere again I ventured near;
I was sick with dread, but I bravely said: "I'll just take a peep inside.
I guess he's cooked, and it's time I looked"; ... then the door I opened wide.

And there sat Sam, looking cool and calm, in the heart of the furnace roar;
And he wore a smile you could see a mile, and he said: "Please close that door.
It's fine in here, but I greatly fear you'll let in the cold and storm—
Since I left Plumtree, down in Tennessee, it's the first time I've been warm."

There are strange things done in the midnight sun
By the men who moil for gold;
The Arctic trails have their secret tales
That would make your blood run cold;
The Northern Lights have seen queer sights,
But the queerest they ever did see
Was that night on the marge of Lake Lebarge
I cremated Sam McGee.

ALL THE WORLD'S A STAGE

by William Shakespeare

All the world's a stage,
And all the men and women merely players;
They have their exits and their entrances;
And one man in his time plays many parts,
His acts being seven ages. At first the infant,
Mewling and puking in the nurse's arms;
And then the whining school-boy, with his satchel
And shining morning face, creeping like snail
Unwillingly to school. And then the lover,
Sighing like furnace, with a woeful ballad
Made to his mistress' eyebrow. Then a soldier,
Full of strange oaths, and bearded like the pard,
Jealous in honour, sudden and quick in quarrel,
Seeking the bubble reputation
Even in the cannon's mouth. And then the justice,
In fair round belly with good capon lin'd,
With eyes severe and beard of formal cut,
Full of wise saws and modern instances;
And so he plays his part. The sixth age shifts
Into the lean and slipper'd pantaloon,
With spectacles on nose and pouch on side;
His youthful hose, well sav'd, a world too wide
For his shrunk shank; and his big manly voice,
Turning again toward childish treble, pipes
And whistles in his sound. Last scene of all,
That ends this strange eventful history,
Is second childishness and mere oblivion;
Sans teeth, sans eyes, sans taste, sans everything.

A FAIRY SONG

by William Shakespeare

Over hill, over dale,
Thorough bush, thorough brier,
Over park, over pale,
Thorough flood, thorough fire!
I do wander everywhere,
Swifter than the moon's sphere;
And I serve the Fairy Queen,
To dew her orbs upon the green;
The cowslips tall her pensioners be;
In their gold coats spots you see;
Those be rubies, fairy favours;
In those freckles live their savours;
I must go seek some dewdrops here,
And hang a pearl in every cowslip's ear.

CARPE DIEM

by William Shakespeare

O mistress mine, where are you roaming?
O stay and hear! your true-love's coming
That can sing both high and low;
Trip no further, pretty sweeting,
Journey's end in lovers' meeting—
Every wise man's son doth know.

What is love? 'tis not hereafter;
Present mirth hath present laughter;
What's to come is still unsure:
In delay there lies no plenty,—
Then come kiss me, sweet and twenty,
Youth's a stuff will not endure.

SONNET 18:
SHALL I COMPARE THEE TO A SUMMER'S DAY?

by William Shakespeare

Shall I compare thee to a summer's day?
    Thou art more lovely and more temperate:
Rough winds do shake the darling buds of May,
    And summer's lease hath all too short a date:
Sometime too hot the eye of heaven shines,
    And often is his gold complexion dimm'd;
And every fair from fair sometime declines,
    By chance, or nature's changing course, untrimm'd;
But thy eternal summer shall not fade,
    Nor lose possession of that fair thou owest;
Nor shall Death brag thou wander'st in his shade,
    When in eternal lines to time thou growest;
So long as men can breathe, or eyes can see,
    So long lives this, and this gives life to thee.

SONNET 20:
A WOMAN'S FACE WITH NATURE'S OWN HAND PAINTED

by William Shakespeare

A woman's face with nature's own hand painted
Hast thou, the master-mistress of my passion;
A woman's gentle heart, but not acquainted
With shifting change as is false women's fashion;
An eye more bright than theirs, less false in rolling,
Gilding the object whereupon it gazeth;
A man in hue, all hues in his controlling,
Which steals men's eyes and women's souls amazeth.
And for a woman wert thou first created,
Till nature as she wrought thee fell a-doting,
And by addition me of thee defeated
By adding one thing to my purpose nothing.
    But since she pricked thee out for women's pleasure,
    Mine be thy love and thy love's use their treasure.

SONNET 29:
WHEN, IN DISGRACE WITH FORTUNE AND MEN'S EYES

by William Shakespeare

When, in disgrace with fortune and men's eyes,
I all alone beweep my outcast state
And trouble deaf heaven with my bootless cries
And look upon myself and curse my fate,
Wishing me like to one more rich in hope,
Featur'd like him, like him with friends possess'd,
Desiring this man's art and that man's scope,
With what I most enjoy contented least;
Yet in these thoughts myself almost despising,
Haply I think on thee, and then my state,
Like to the lark at break of day arising
From sullen earth, sings hymns at heaven's gate;
  For thy sweet love remember'd such wealth brings
  That then I scorn to change my state with kings.

SONNET 73:
THAT TIME OF YEAR THOU MAYST IN ME BEHOLD

by William Shakespeare

That time of year thou mayst in me behold
When yellow leaves, or none, or few, do hang
Upon those boughs which shake against the cold,
Bare ruin'd choirs, where late the sweet birds sang.

In me thou see'st the twilight of such day
As after sunset fadeth in the west,
Which by and by black night doth take away,
Death's second self, that seals up all in rest.

In me thou see'st the glowing of such fire
That on the ashes of his youth doth lie,
As the death-bed whereon it must expire,
Consum'd with that which it was nourish'd by.

This thou perceiv'st, which makes thy love more strong,
To love that well which thou must leave ere long.

SONNET 116:
LET ME NOT TO THE MARRIAGE OF TRUE MINDS

by William Shakespeare

Let me not to the marriage of true minds
Admit impediments. Love is not love
Which alters when it alteration finds,
Or bends with the remover to remove.
O no! it is an ever-fixed mark
That looks on tempests and is never shaken;
It is the star to every wand'ring bark,
Whose worth's unknown, although his height be taken.
Love's not Time's fool, though rosy lips and cheeks
Within his bending sickle's compass come;
Love alters not with his brief hours and weeks,
But bears it out even to the edge of doom.
If this be error and upon me prov'd,
I never writ, nor no man ever lov'd.

SONNET 130:
MY MISTRESS' EYES ARE NOTHING LIKE THE SUN

by William Shakespeare

My mistress' eyes are nothing like the sun;
Coral is far more red than her lips' red;
If snow be white, why then her breasts are dun;
If hairs be wires, black wires grow on her head.
I have seen roses damasked, red and white,
But no such roses see I in her cheeks;
And in some perfumes is there more delight
Than in the breath that from my mistress reeks.
I love to hear her speak, yet well I know
That music hath a far more pleasing sound;
I grant I never saw a goddess go;
My mistress, when she walks, treads on the ground.
  And yet, by heaven, I think my love as rare
  As any she belied with false compare.

OZYMANDIAS

by Percy Bysshe Shelley

I met a traveller from an antique land
Who said: "Two vast and trunkless legs of stone
Stand in the desert. Near them on the sand,
Half sunk, a shattered visage lies, whose frown
And wrinkled lip and sneer of cold command
Tell that its sculptor well those passions read
Which yet survive, stamped on these lifeless things,
The hand that mock'd them and the heart that fed;
And on the pedestal these words appear:
'My name is Ozymandias, king of kings:
Look on my works, ye Mighty, and despair!'
Nothing beside remains. Round the decay
Of that colossal wreck, boundless and bare,
The lone and level sands stretch far away;"

ODE TO THE WEST WIND

by Percy Bysshe Shelley

I

O wild West Wind, thou breath of Autumn's being,
Thou, from whose unseen presence the leaves dead
Are driven, like ghosts from an enchanter fleeing,

Yellow, and black, and pale, and hectic red,
Pestilence-stricken multitudes: O thou,
Who chariotest to their dark wintry bed

The winged seeds, where they lie cold and low,
Each like a corpse within its grave, until
Thine azure sister of the Spring shall blow

Her clarion o'er the dreaming earth, and fill
(Driving sweet buds like flocks to feed in air)
With living hues and odours plain and hill:

Wild Spirit, which art moving everywhere;
Destroyer and preserver; hear, oh hear!

II

Thou on whose stream, mid the steep sky's commotion,
Loose clouds like earth's decaying leaves are shed,
Shook from the tangled boughs of Heaven and Ocean,

Angels of rain and lightning: there are spread
On the blue surface of thine aëry surge,
Like the bright hair uplifted from the head

Of some fierce Maenad, even from the dim verge
Of the horizon to the zenith's height,
The locks of the approaching storm. Thou dirge

Of the dying year, to which this closing night
Will be the dome of a vast sepulchre,
Vaulted with all thy congregated might

Of vapours, from whose solid atmosphere
Black rain, and fire, and hail will burst: oh hear!

III

Thou who didst waken from his summer dreams
The blue Mediterranean, where he lay,
Lull'd by the coil of his crystalline streams,

Beside a pumice isle in Baiae's bay,
And saw in sleep old palaces and towers
Quivering within the wave's intenser day,

All overgrown with azure moss and flowers
So sweet, the sense faints picturing them! Thou
For whose path the Atlantic's level powers

Cleave themselves into chasms, while far below
The sea-blooms and the oozy woods which wear
The sapless foliage of the ocean, know

Thy voice, and suddenly grow gray with fear,
And tremble and despoil themselves: oh hear!

IV

If I were a dead leaf thou mightest bear;
If I were a swift cloud to fly with thee;
A wave to pant beneath thy power, and share

The impulse of thy strength, only less free
Than thou, O uncontrollable! If even
I were as in my boyhood, and could be

The impulse of thy strength, only less free
Than thou, O uncontrollable! If even
I were as in my boyhood, and could be

As thus with thee in prayer in my sore need.
Oh, lift me as a wave, a leaf, a cloud!
I fall upon the thorns of life! I bleed!

A heavy weight of hours has chain'd and bow'd
One too like thee: tameless, and swift, and proud.

V

Make me thy lyre, even as the forest is:
What if my leaves are falling like its own!
The tumult of thy mighty harmonies

Will take from both a deep, autumnal tone,
Sweet though in sadness. Be thou, Spirit fierce,
My spirit! Be thou me, impetuous one!

Drive my dead thoughts over the universe
Like wither'd leaves to quicken a new birth!
And, by the incantation of this verse,

Drive my dead thoughts over the universe
Like wither'd leaves to quicken a new birth!
And, by the incantation of this verse,

The trumpet of a prophecy! O Wind,
If Winter comes, can Spring be far behind?

TO A SKYLARK

by Percy Bysshe Shelley

Hail to thee, blithe Spirit!
   Bird thou never wert,
That from Heaven, or near it,
   Pourest thy full heart
In profuse strains of unpremeditated art.

Higher still and higher
   From the earth thou springest
Like a cloud of fire;
   The blue deep thou wingest,
And singing still dost soar, and soaring ever singest.

In the golden lightning
   Of the sunken sun
O'er which clouds are bright'ning,
   Thou dost float and run,
Like an unbodied joy whose race is just begun.

The pale purple even
   Melts around thy flight;
Like a star of Heaven
   In the broad daylight
Thou art unseen, but yet I hear thy shrill delight:

Keen as are the arrows
   Of that silver sphere,
Whose intense lamp narrows
   In the white dawn clear
Until we hardly see — we feel that it is there.

All the earth and air
   With thy voice is loud.
As, when night is bare,
   From one lonely cloud
The moon rains out her beams, and heaven is overflowed.

What thou art we know not;
   What is most like thee?
From rainbow clouds there flow not
   Drops so bright to see
As from thy presence showers a rain of melody.

Like a poet hidden
   In the light of thought,
Singing hymns unbidden,
   Till the world is wrought
To sympathy with hopes and fears it heeded not:

Like a high-born maiden
   In a palace tower,
Soothing her love-laden
   Soul in secret hour
With music sweet as love, which overflows her bower:

Like a glow-worm golden
   In a dell of dew,
Scattering unbeholden
   Its aerial hue
Among the flowers and grass, which screen it from the view:

251

Like a rose embowered
    In its own green leaves,
By warm winds deflowered,
    Till the scent it gives
Makes faint with too much sweet these heavy-winged thieves.

Sound of vernal showers
    On the twinkling grass,
Rain-awakened flowers,
    All that ever was
Joyous, and clear, and fresh, thy music doth surpass.

Teach us, sprite or bird,
    What sweet thoughts are thine:
I have never heard
    Praise of love or wine
That panted forth a flood of rapture so divine.

Chorus hymeneal
    Or triumphal chaunt
Matched with thine, would be all
    But an empty vaunt —
A thing wherein we feel there is some hidden want.

What objects are the fountains
    Of thy happy strain?
What fields, or waves, or mountains?
    What shapes of sky or plain?
What love of thine own kind? what ignorance of pain?

With thy clear keen joyance
    Languor cannot be:
Shadow of annoyance
    Never came near thee:
Thou lovest, but ne'er knew love's sad satiety.

Waking or asleep,
    Thou of death must deem
Things more true and deep
    Than we mortals dream,
Or how could thy notes flow in such a crystal stream?

We look before and after,
    And pine for what is not:
Our sincerest laughter
    With some pain is fraught;
Our sweetest songs are those that tell of saddest thought.

Yet if we could scorn
    Hate, and pride, and fear;
If we were things born
    Not to shed a tear,
I know not how thy joy we ever should come near.

Better than all measures
    Of delightful sound,
Better than all treasures
    That in books are found,
Thy skill to poet were, thou scorner of the ground!

Teach me half the gladness
    That thy brain must know,
Such harmonious madness
    From my lips would flow
The world should listen then, as I am listening now!

MY LOVE IS LIKE TO ICE

by Edmund Spenser

My love is like to ice, and I to fire:
How comes it then that this her cold so great
Is not dissolved through my so hot desire,
But harder grows the more I her entreat?
Or how comes it that my exceeding heat
Is not allayed by her heart-frozen cold,
But that I burn much more in boiling sweat,
And feel my flames augmented manifold?
What more miraculous thing may be told,
That fire, which all things melts, should harden ice,
And ice, which is congeal'd with senseless cold,
Should kindle fire by wonderful device?
Such is the power of love in gentle mind,
That it can alter all the course of kind.

SACRED EMILY

by Gertrude Stein

Rose is a rose is a rose is a rose
Loveliness extreme.
Extra gaiters,
Loveliness extreme
Sweetest ice-cream.
Pages ages page ages page ages.

THIRTEEN WAYS OF LOOKING AT A BLACKBIRD

by Wallace Stevens

I
Among twenty snowy mountains,
The only moving thing
Was the eye of the blackbird.

II
I was of three minds,
Like a tree
In which there are three blackbirds.

III
The blackbird whirled in the autumn winds.
It was a small part of the pantomime.

IV
A man and a woman
Are one.
A man and a woman and a blackbird
Are one.

V
I do not know which to prefer,
The beauty of inflections
Or the beauty of innuendoes,
The blackbird whistling
Or just after.

VI
Icicles filled the long window
With barbaric glass.
The shadow of the blackbird
Crossed it, to and fro.
The mood
Traced in the shadow
An indecipherable cause.

VII
O thin men of Haddam,
Why do you imagine golden birds?
Do you not see how the blackbird
Walks around the feet
Of the women about you?

VIII
I know noble accents
And lucid, inescapable rhythms;
But I know, too,
That the blackbird is involved
In what I know.

IX
When the blackbird flew out of sight,
It marked the edge
Of one of many circles.

X
At the sight of blackbirds
Flying in a green light,
Even the bawds of euphony
Would cry out sharply.

XI
He rode over Connecticut
In a glass coach.
Once, a fear pierced him,
In that he mistook
The shadow of his equipage
For blackbirds.

XII
The river is moving.
The blackbird must be flying.

XIII
It was evening all afternoon.
It was snowing
And it was going to snow.
The blackbird sat
In the cedar-limbs.

MY SHADOW

by Robert Louis Stevenson

I have a little shadow that goes in and out with me,
And what can be the use of him is more than I can see.
He is very, very like me from the heels up to the head;
And I see him jump before me, when I jump into my bed.

The funniest thing about him is the way he likes to grow—
Not at all like proper children, which is always very slow;
For he sometimes shoots up taller like an India-rubber ball,
And he sometimes gets so little that there's none of him at all.

He hasn't got a notion of how children ought to play,
And can only make a fool of me in every sort of way.
He stays so close beside me, he's a coward you can see;
I'd think shame to stick to nursie as that shadow sticks to me!

One morning, very early, before the sun was up,
I rose and found the shining dew on every buttercup;
But my lazy little shadow, like an arrant sleepy-head,
Had stayed at home behind me and was fast asleep in bed.

BREAK, BREAK, BREAK

by Alfred, Lord Tennyson

Break, break, break,
    On thy cold gray stones, O sea!
And I would that my tongue could utter
    The thoughts that arise in me.

Oh, well for the fisherman's boy,
    That he shouts with his sister at play!
Oh, well for the sailor lad,
    That he sings in his boat on the bay!

And the stately ships go on
    To their haven under the hill;
But oh for the touch of a vanished hand,
    And the sound of a voice that is still!

Break, break, break,
    At the foot of thy crags, O sea!
But the tender grace of a day that is dead
    Will never come back to me.

CROSSING THE BAR

by Alfred, Lord Tennyson

Sunset and evening star,
    And one clear call for me!
And may there be no moaning of the bar,
    When I put out to sea,

But such a tide as moving seems asleep,
    Too full for sound and foam,
When that which drew from out the boundless deep
    Turns again home.

Twilight and evening bell,
    And after that the dark!
And may there be no sadness of farewell,
    When I embark;

For tho' from out our bourne of Time and Place
    The flood may bear me far,
I hope to see my Pilot face to face
    When I have crost the bar.

IN MEMORIAM A.H.H.

by Alfred, Lord Tennyson

Ring out, wild bells, to the wild sky,
    The flying cloud, the frosty light:
    The year is dying in the night;
Ring out, wild bells, and let him die.

Ring out the old, ring in the new,
    Ring, happy bells, across the snow:
    The year is going, let him go;
Ring out the false, ring in the true.

Ring out the grief that saps the mind
    For those that here we see no more;
    Ring out the feud of rich and poor,
Ring in redress to all mankind.

Ring out a slowly dying cause,
    And ancient forms of party strife;
    Ring in the nobler modes of life,
With sweeter manners, purer laws.

Ring out the want, the care, the sin,
    The faithless coldness of the times;
    Ring out, ring out my mournful rhymes
But ring the fuller minstrel in.

Ring out false pride in place and blood,
  The civic slander and the spite;
  Ring in the love of truth and right,
Ring in the common love of good.

Ring out old shapes of foul disease;
  Ring out the narrowing lust of gold;
  Ring out the thousand wars of old,
Ring in the thousand years of peace.

Ring in the valiant man and free,
  The larger heart, the kindlier hand;
  Ring out the darkness of the land,
Ring in the Christ that is to be.

THE CHARGE OF THE LIGHT BRIGADE

by Alfred, Lord Tennyson

Half a league, half a league,
Half a league onward,
All in the valley of Death
   Rode the six hundred.
"Forward, the Light Brigade!
Charge for the guns!" he said.
Into the valley of Death
   Rode the six hundred.

"Forward, the Light Brigade!"
Was there a man dismayed?
Not though the soldier knew
   Someone had blundered.
   Theirs not to make reply,
   Theirs not to reason why,
   Theirs but to do and die.
   Into the valley of Death
   Rode the six hundred.

Cannon to right of them,
Cannon to left of them,
Cannon in front of them
   Volleyed and thundered;
Stormed at with shot and shell,
Boldly they rode and well,
Into the jaws of Death,
Into the mouth of hell
   Rode the six hundred.

Flashed all their sabres bare,
Flashed as they turned in air
Sabring the gunners there,
Charging an army, while
 All the world wondered.
Plunged in the battery-smoke
Right through the line they broke;
Cossack and Russian
Reeled from the sabre stroke
 Shattered and sundered.
Then they rode back, but not
 Not the six hundred.

Cannon to right of them,
Cannon to left of them,
Cannon behind them
 Volleyed and thundered;
Stormed at with shot and shell,
While horse and hero fell.
They that had fought so well
Came through the jaws of Death,
Back from the mouth of hell,
All that was left of them,
 Left of six hundred.

When can their glory fade?
O the wild charge they made!
 All the world wondered.
Honour the charge they made!
Honour the Light Brigade,
 Noble six hundred!

THE LADY OF SHALOTT

by Alfred, Lord Tennyson

Part I

On either side the river lie
Long fields of barley and of rye,
That clothe the wold and meet the sky;
And thro' the field the road runs by
    To many-tower'd Camelot;
The yellow-leaved waterlily
The green-sheathed daffodilly
Tremble in the water chilly
   Round about Shalott.

Willows whiten, aspens shiver.
The sunbeam showers break and quiver
In the stream that runneth ever
By the island in the river
    Flowing down to Camelot.
Four gray walls, and four gray towers
Overlook a space of flowers,
And the silent isle imbowers
   The Lady of Shalott.

Underneath the bearded barley,
The reaper, reaping late and early,
Hears her ever chanting cheerly,
Like an angel, singing clearly,
   O'er the stream of Camelot.

Piling the sheaves in furrows airy,
Beneath the moon, the reaper weary
Listening whispers, ' 'Tis the fairy,
     Lady of Shalott.'

The little isle is all inrail'd
With a rose-fence, and overtrail'd
With roses: by the marge unhail'd
The shallop flitteth silken sail'd,
Skimming down to Camelot.
A pearl garland winds her head:
She leaneth on a velvet bed,
Full royally apparelled,
The Lady of Shalott.

Part II

No time hath she to sport and play:
A charmed web she weaves alway.
A curse is on her, if she stay
Her weaving, either night or day,
     To look down to Camelot.
She knows not what the curse may be;
Therefore she weaveth steadily,
Therefore no other care hath she,
     The Lady of Shalott.

She lives with little joy or fear.
Over the water, running near,
The sheepbell tinkles in her ear.
Before her hangs a mirror clear,
     Reflecting tower'd Camelot.
And as the mazy web she whirls,
She sees the surly village churls,
And the red cloaks of market girls
     Pass onward from Shalott.

Sometimes a troop of damsels glad,
An abbot on an ambling pad,
Sometimes a curly shepherd lad,
Or long-hair'd page in crimson clad,
    Goes by to tower'd Camelot:
And sometimes thro' the mirror blue
The knights come riding two and two:
She hath no loyal knight and true,
    The Lady of Shalott.

But in her web she still delights
To weave the mirror's magic sights,
For often thro' the silent nights
A funeral, with plumes and lights
    And music, came from Camelot:
Or when the moon was overhead
Came two young lovers lately wed;
I am half sick of shadows,' said
    The Lady of Shalott.

Part III

A bow-shot from her bower-eaves,
He rode between the barley-sheaves,
The sun came dazzling thro' the leaves,
And flam'd upon the brazen greaves
    Of bold Sir Lancelot.
A red-cross knight for ever kneel'd
To a lady in his shield,
That sparkled on the yellow field,
    Beside remote Shalott.

The gemmy bridle glitter'd free,
Like to some branch of stars we see
Hung in the golden Galaxy.
The bridle bells rang merrily
As he rode down from Camelot:

And from his blazon'd baldric slung
A mighty silver bugle hung,
And as he rode his armour rung,
Beside remote Shalott.

All in the blue unclouded weather
Thick-jewell'd shone the saddle-leather,
The helmet and the helmet-feather
Burn'd like one burning flame together,
    As he rode down from Camelot.
As often thro' the purple night,
Below the starry clusters bright,
Some bearded meteor, trailing light,
    Moves over green Shalott.

His broad clear brow in sunlight glow'd;
On burnish'd hooves his war-horse trode;
From underneath his helmet flow'd
His coal-black curls as on he rode,
    As he rode down from Camelot.
From the bank and from the river
He flash'd into the crystal mirror,
'Tirra lirra, tirra lirra:'
    Sang Sir Lancelot.

She left the web, she left the loom
She made three paces thro' the room
She saw the water-flower bloom,
She saw the helmet and the plume,
    She look'd down to Camelot.
Out flew the web and floated wide;
The mirror crack'd from side to side;
'The curse is come upon me,' cried
    The Lady of Shalott.

Part IV

In the stormy east-wind straining,
The pale yellow woods were waning,
The broad stream in his banks
complaining,
Heavily the low sky raining
    Over tower'd Camelot;
Outside the isle a shallow boat
Beneath a willow lay afloat,
Below the carven stern she wrote,
    The Lady of Shalott.

A cloudwhite crown of pearl she dight,
All raimented in snowy white
That loosely flew (her zone in sight
Clasp'd with one blinding diamond bright)
    Her wide eyes fix'd on Camelot,
Though the squally east-wind keenly
Blew, with folded arms serenely
By the water stood the queenly
    Lady of Shalott.

With a steady stony glance—
Like some bold seer in a trance,
Beholding all his own mischance,
Mute, with a glassy countenance—
    She look'd down to Camelot.
It was the closing of the day:
She loos'd the chain, and down she lay;
The broad stream bore her far away,
    The Lady of Shalott.

As when to sailors while they roam,
By creeks and outfalls far from home,
Rising and dropping with the foam,

From dying swans wild warblings come,
    Blown shoreward; so to Camelot
Still as the boathead wound along
The willowy hills and fields among,
They heard her chanting her deathsong,
    The Lady of Shalott.

A longdrawn carol, mournful, holy,
She chanted loudly, chanted lowly,
Till her eyes were darken'd wholly,
And her smooth face sharpen'd slowly,
    Turn'd to tower'd Camelot:
For ere she reach'd upon the tide
The first house by the water-side,
Singing in her song she died,
    The Lady of Shalott.

Under tower and balcony,
By garden wall and gallery,
A pale, pale corpse she floated by,
Deadcold, between the houses high,
    Dead into tower'd Camelot.
Knight and burgher, lord and dame,
To the planked wharfage came:
Below the stern they read her name,
    The Lady of Shalott.

They cross'd themselves, their stars they blest,
Knight, minstrel, abbot, squire, and guest.
There lay a parchment on her breast,
That puzzled more than all the rest,
    The wellfed wits at Camelot.
'The web was woven curiously,
The charm is broken utterly,
Draw near and fear not,—this is I,
    The Lady of Shalott.'

ULYSSES

by Alfred, Lord Tennyson

It little profits that an idle king,
By this still hearth, among these barren crags,
Match'd with an aged wife, I mete and dole
Unequal laws unto a savage race,
That hoard, and sleep, and feed, and know not me.
I cannot rest from travel: I will drink
Life to the lees: All times I have enjoy'd
Greatly, have suffer'd greatly, both with those
That loved me, and alone, on shore, and when
Thro' scudding drifts the rainy Hyades
Vext the dim sea: I am become a name;
For always roaming with a hungry heart
Much have I seen and known; cities of men
And manners, climates, councils, governments,
Myself not least, but honour'd of them all;
And drunk delight of battle with my peers,
Far on the ringing plains of windy Troy.
I am a part of all that I have met;
Yet all experience is an arch wherethro'
Gleams that untravell'd world whose margin fades
For ever and forever when I move.
How dull it is to pause, to make an end,
To rust unburnish'd, not to shine in use!
As tho' to breathe were life! Life piled on life
Were all too little, and of one to me
Little remains: but every hour is saved

From that eternal silence, something more,
A bringer of new things; and vile it were
For some three suns to store and hoard myself,
And this gray spirit yearning in desire
To follow knowledge like a sinking star,
Beyond the utmost bound of human thought.

     This is my son, mine own Telemachus,
To whom I leave the sceptre and the isle,—
Well-loved of me, discerning to fulfil
This labour, by slow prudence to make mild
A rugged people, and thro' soft degrees
Subdue them to the useful and the good.
Most blameless is he, centred in the sphere
Of common duties, decent not to fail
In offices of tenderness, and pay
Meet adoration to my household gods,
When I am gone. He works his work, I mine.

     There lies the port; the vessel puffs her sail:
There gloom the dark, broad seas. My mariners,
Souls that have toil'd, and wrought, and thought with me—
That ever with a frolic welcome took
The thunder and the sunshine, and opposed
Free hearts, free foreheads—you and I are old;
Old age hath yet his honour and his toil;
Death closes all: but something ere the end,
Some work of noble note, may yet be done,
Not unbecoming men that strove with Gods.
The lights begin to twinkle from the rocks:
The long day wanes: the slow moon climbs: the deep
Moans round with many voices. Come, my friends,
'T is not too late to seek a newer world.
Push off, and sitting well in order smite

The sounding furrows; for my purpose holds
To sail beyond the sunset, and the baths
Of all the western stars, until I die.
It may be that the gulfs will wash us down:
It may be we shall touch the Happy Isles,
And see the great Achilles, whom we knew.
Tho' much is taken, much abides; and tho'
We are not now that strength which in old days
Moved earth and heaven, that which we are, we are;
One equal temper of heroic hearts,
Made weak by time and fate, but strong in will
To strive, to seek, to find, and not to yield.

FRIENDSHIP

by *Henry David Thoreau*

I think awhile of Love, and while I think,
  Love is to me a world,
  Sole meat and sweetest drink,
  And close connecting link
   Tween heaven and earth.

I only know it is, not how or why,
  My greatest happiness;
  However hard I try,
  Not if I were to die,
   Can I explain.

I fain would ask my friend how it can be,
  But when the time arrives,
  Then Love is more lovely
  Than anything to me,
   And so I'm dumb.

For if the truth were known, Love cannot speak,
  But only thinks and does;
  Though surely out 'twill leak
  Without the help of Greek,
   Or any tongue.

A man may love the truth and practise it,
  Beauty he may admire,
  And goodness not omit,
  As much as may befit
   To reverence.

But only when these three together meet,
    As they always incline,
    And make one soul the seat,
    And favorite retreat,
        Of loveliness;

When under kindred shape, like loves and hates
    And a kindred nature,
    Proclaim us to be mates,
    Exposed to equal fates
        Eternally;

And each may other help, and service do,
    Drawing Love's bands more tight,
    Service he ne'er shall rue
    While one and one make two,
        And two are one;

In such case only doth man fully prove
    Fully as man can do,
    What power there is in Love
    His inmost soul to move
        Resistlessly.

        —

Two sturdy oaks I mean, which side by side,
    Withstand the winter's storm,
    And spite of wind and tide,
    Grow up the meadow's pride,
        For both are strong

Above they barely touch, but undermined
    Down to their deepest source,
    Admiring you shall find
    Their roots are intertwined
        Insep'rably.

I SING THE BODY ELECTRIC

by Walt Whitman

1

I sing the body electric,
The armies of those I love engirth me and I engirth them,
They will not let me off till I go with them, respond to them,
And discorrupt them, and charge them full with the charge of the soul.

Was it doubted that those who corrupt their own bodies conceal themselves?
And if those who defile the living are as bad as they who defile the dead?
And if the body does not do fully as much as the soul?
And if the body were not the soul, what is the soul?

2

The love of the body of man or woman balks account, the body itself balks account,
That of the male is perfect, and that of the female is perfect.

The expression of the face balks account,
But the expression of a well-made man appears not only in his face,
It is in his limbs and joints also, it is curiously in the joints of his hips and wrists,
It is in his walk, the carriage of his neck, the flex of his waist and knees, dress does not hide him,
The strong sweet quality he has strikes through the cotton and broadcloth,
To see him pass conveys as much as the best poem, perhaps more,
You linger to see his back, and the back of his neck and shoulder-side.

The sprawl and fulness of babes, the bosoms and heads of women, the folds of their dress, their style as we pass in the street, the contour of their shape downwards,
The swimmer naked in the swimming-bath, seen as he swims through the transparent green-shine, or lies with his face up and rolls silently to and fro in the heave of the water,
The bending forward and backward of rowers in row-boats, the horseman in his saddle,
Girls, mothers, house-keepers, in all their performances,

The group of laborers seated at noon-time with their open dinner-kettles, and their wives waiting,
The female soothing a child, the farmer's daughter in the garden or cow-yard,
The young fellow hoeing corn, the sleigh-driver driving his six horses through the crowd,
The wrestle of wrestlers, two apprentice-boys, quite grown, lusty, good-natured, native-born, out on the vacant lot at sun-down after work,
The coats and caps thrown down, the embrace of love and resistance,
The upper-hold and under-hold, the hair rumpled over and blinding the eyes;
The march of firemen in their own costumes, the play of masculine muscle through clean-setting trowsers and waist-straps,
The slow return from the fire, the pause when the bell strikes suddenly again, and the listening on the alert,
The natural, perfect, varied attitudes, the bent head, the curv'd neck and the counting;
Such-like I love—I loosen myself, pass freely, am at the mother's breast with the little child,
Swim with the swimmers, wrestle with wrestlers, march in line with the firemen, and pause, listen, count.

3
I knew a man, a common farmer, the father of five sons,
And in them the fathers of sons, and in them the fathers of sons.

This man was of wonderful vigor, calmness, beauty of person,
The shape of his head, the pale yellow and white of his hair and beard, the immeasurable meaning of his black eyes, the richness and breadth of his manners,
These I used to go and visit him to see, he was wise also,
He was six feet tall, he was over eighty years old, his sons were massive, clean, bearded, tan-faced, handsome,
They and his daughters loved him, all who saw him loved him,
They did not love him by allowance, they loved him with personal love,
He drank water only, the blood show'd like scarlet through the clear-brown skin of his face,
He was a frequent gunner and fisher, he sail'd his boat himself, he had a fine one presented to him by a ship-joiner, he had fowling-pieces presented to him by men that loved him,
When he went with his five sons and many grand-sons to hunt or fish, you would pick him out as the most beautiful and vigorous of the gang,
You would wish long and long to be with him, you would wish to sit by him in the boat that you and he might touch each other.

4

I have perceiv'd that to be with those I like is enough,
To stop in company with the rest at evening is enough,
To be surrounded by beautiful, curious, breathing, laughing flesh is enough,
To pass among them or touch any one, or rest my arm ever so lightly round his or her neck for a moment, what is this then?
I do not ask any more delight, I swim in it as in a sea.

There is something in staying close to men and women and looking on them, and in the contact and odor of them, that pleases the soul well,
All things please the soul, but these please the soul well.

5

This is the female form,
A divine nimbus exhales from it from head to foot,
It attracts with fierce undeniable attraction,
I am drawn by its breath as if I were no more than a helpless vapor, all falls aside but myself and it,
Books, art, religion, time, the visible and solid earth, and what was expected of heaven or fear'd of hell, are now consumed,
Mad filaments, ungovernable shoots play out of it, the response likewise ungovernable,
Hair, bosom, hips, bend of legs, negligent falling hands all diffused, mine too diffused,
Ebb stung by the flow and flow stung by the ebb, love-flesh swelling and deliciously aching,
Limitless limpid jets of love hot and enormous, quivering jelly of love, white-blow and delirious juice,
Bridegroom night of love working surely and softly into the prostrate dawn,
Undulating into the willing and yielding day,
Lost in the cleave of the clasping and sweet-flesh'd day.

This the nucleus—after the child is born of woman, man is born of woman,
This the bath of birth, this the merge of small and large, and the outlet again.

Be not ashamed women, your privilege encloses the rest, and is the exit of the rest,
You are the gates of the body, and you are the gates of the soul.

The female contains all qualities and tempers them,
She is in her place and moves with perfect balance,
She is all things duly veil'd, she is both passive and active,
She is to conceive daughters as well as sons, and sons as well as daughters.

As I see my soul reflected in Nature,
As I see through a mist, One with inexpressible completeness, sanity, beauty,
See the bent head and arms folded over the breast, the Female I see.

6

The male is not less the soul nor more, he too is in his place,
He too is all qualities, he is action and power,
The flush of the known universe is in him,
Scorn becomes him well, and appetite and defiance become him well,
The wildest largest passions, bliss that is utmost, sorrow that is utmost become him well, pride is for him,
The full-spread pride of man is calming and excellent to the soul,
Knowledge becomes him, he likes it always, he brings every thing to the test of himself,
Whatever the survey, whatever the sea and the sail he strikes soundings at last only here,
(Where else does he strike soundings except here?)

The man's body is sacred and the woman's body is sacred,
No matter who it is, it is sacred—is it the meanest one in the laborers' gang?
Is it one of the dull-faced immigrants just landed on the wharf?
Each belongs here or anywhere just as much as the well-off, just as much as you,
Each has his or her place in the procession.

(All is a procession,
The universe is a procession with measured and perfect motion.)

Do you know so much yourself that you call the meanest ignorant?
Do you suppose you have a right to a good sight, and he or she has no right to a sight?
Do you think matter has cohered together from its diffuse float, and the soil is on the surface, and water runs and vegetation sprouts,
For you only, and not for him and her?

7

A man's body at auction,
(For before the war I often go to the slave-mart and watch the sale,)
I help the auctioneer, the sloven does not half know his business.

Gentlemen look on this wonder,
Whatever the bids of the bidders they cannot be high enough for it,
For it the globe lay preparing quintillions of years without one animal or plant,
For it the revolving cycles truly and steadily roll'd.

In this head the all-baffling brain,
In it and below it the makings of heroes.

Examine these limbs, red, black, or white, they are cunning in tendon and nerve,
They shall be stript that you may see them.

Exquisite senses, life-lit eyes, pluck, volition,
Flakes of breast-muscle, pliant backbone and neck, flesh not flabby, good-sized arms and legs,
And wonders within there yet.

Within there runs blood,
The same old blood! the same red-running blood!
There swells and jets a heart, there all passions, desires, reachings, aspirations,
(Do you think they are not there because they are not express'd in parlors and lecture-rooms?)

This is not only one man, this the father of those who shall be fathers in their turns,
In him the start of populous states and rich republics,
Of him countless immortal lives with countless embodiments and enjoyments.

How do you know who shall come from the offspring of his offspring through the centuries?
(Who might you find you have come from yourself, if you could trace back through the centuries?)

8

A woman's body at auction,
She too is not only herself, she is the teeming mother of mothers,
She is the bearer of them that shall grow and be mates to the mothers.

Have you ever loved the body of a woman?
Have you ever loved the body of a man?
Do you not see that these are exactly the same to all in all nations and times all over the earth?

If any thing is sacred the human body is sacred,
And the glory and sweet of a man is the token of manhood untainted,
And in man or woman a clean, strong, firm-fibred body, is more beautiful than the most beautiful face.

Have you seen the fool that corrupted his own live body? or the fool that corrupted her own live body?
For they do not conceal themselves, and cannot conceal themselves.

9

O my body! I dare not desert the likes of you in other men and women, nor the likes of the parts of you,
I believe the likes of you are to stand or fall with the likes of the soul, (and that they are the soul,)
I believe the likes of you shall stand or fall with my poems, and that they are my poems,
Man's, woman's, child's, youth's, wife's, husband's, mother's, father's, young man's, young woman's poems,
Head, neck, hair, ears, drop and tympan of the ears,
Eyes, eye-fringes, iris of the eye, eyebrows, and the waking or sleeping of the lids,
Mouth, tongue, lips, teeth, roof of the mouth, jaws, and the jaw-hinges,
Nose, nostrils of the nose, and the partition,
Cheeks, temples, forehead, chin, throat, back of the neck, neck-slue,
Strong shoulders, manly beard, scapula, hind-shoulders, and the ample side-round of the chest,
Upper-arm, armpit, elbow-socket, lower-arm, arm-sinews, arm-bones,
Wrist and wrist-joints, hand, palm, knuckles, thumb, forefinger, finger-joints, finger-nails,
Broad breast-front, curling hair of the breast, breast-bone, breast-side,
Ribs, belly, backbone, joints of the backbone,
Hips, hip-sockets, hip-strength, inward and outward round, man-balls, man-root,

Strong set of thighs, well carrying the trunk above,
Leg fibres, knee, knee-pan, upper-leg, under-leg,
Ankles, instep, foot-ball, toes, toe-joints, the heel;
All attitudes, all the shapeliness, all the belongings of my or your body or of any one's body, male or female,
The lung-sponges, the stomach-sac, the bowels sweet and clean,
The brain in its folds inside the skull-frame,
Sympathies, heart-valves, palate-valves, sexuality, maternity,
Womanhood, and all that is a woman, and the man that comes from woman,
The womb, the teats, nipples, breast-milk, tears, laughter, weeping, love-looks, love-perturbations and risings,
The voice, articulation, language, whispering, shouting aloud,
Food, drink, pulse, digestion, sweat, sleep, walking, swimming,
Poise on the hips, leaping, reclining, embracing, arm-curving and tightening,
The continual changes of the flex of the mouth, and around the eyes,
The skin, the sunburnt shade, freckles, hair,
The curious sympathy one feels when feeling with the hand the naked meat of the body,
The circling rivers the breath, and breathing it in and out,
The beauty of the waist, and thence of the hips, and thence downward toward the knees,
The thin red jellies within you or within me, the bones and the marrow in the bones,
The exquisite realization of health;
O I say these are not the parts and poems of the body only, but of the soul,
O I say now these are the soul!

O CAPTAIN! MY CAPTAIN!

by Walt Whitman

O Captain! My Captain! our fearful trip is done;
The ship has weather'd every rack, the prize we sought is won;
The port is near, the bells I hear, the people all exulting,
While follow eyes the steady keel, the vessel grim and daring:

But O heart! heart! heart!
O the bleeding drops of red,
Where on the deck my Captain lies,
Fallen cold and dead.

O Captain! my Captain! rise up and hear the bells;
Rise up—for you the flag is flung—for you the bugle trills;
For you bouquets and ribbon'd wreaths—for you the shores a-crowding;
For you they call, the swaying mass, their eager faces turning;

O captain! dear father!
This arm beneath your head;
It is some dream that on the deck,
You've fallen cold and dead.

My Captain does not answer, his lips are pale and still;
My father does not feel my arm, he has no pulse nor will;
The ship is anchor'd safe and sound, its voyage closed and done;
From fearful trip, the victor ship, comes in with object won;

Exult, O shores, and ring, O bells!
But I, with mournful tread,
Walk the deck my captain lies,
Fallen cold and dead.

O ME! O LIFE!
by Walt Whitman

Oh me! Oh life! of the questions of these recurring,
Of the endless trains of the faithless, of cities fill'd with the foolish,
Of myself forever reproaching myself, (for who more foolish than I, and who more faithless?)
Of eyes that vainly crave the light, of the objects mean, of the struggle ever renew'd,
Of the poor results of all, of the plodding and sordid crowds I see around me,
Of the empty and useless years of the rest, with the rest me intertwined,
The question, O me! so sad, recurring—What good amid these, O me, O life?

Answer.
That you are here—that life exists and identity,
That the powerful play goes on, and you may contribute a verse.

PIONEERS! O PIONEERS!

by Walt Whitman

Come, my tan-faced children,
Follow well in order, get your weapons ready;
Have you your pistols? have you your sharp edged axes?
Pioneers! O pioneers!

For we cannot tarry here,
We must march my darlings, we must bear the brunt of danger,
We, the youthful sinewy races, all the rest on us depend,
Pioneers! O pioneers!

O you youths, western youths,
So impatient, full of action, full of manly pride and friendship,
Plain I see you, western youths, see you tramping with the foremost,
Pioneers! O pioneers!

Have the elder races halted?
Do they droop and end their lesson, wearied, over there beyond the seas?
We take up the task eternal, and the burden, and the lesson,
Pioneers! O pioneers!

All the past we leave behind;
We debouch upon a newer, mightier world, varied world,
Fresh and strong the world we seize, world of labor and the march,
Pioneers! O pioneers!

We detachments steady throwing,
Down the edges, through the passes, up the mountains steep,
Conquering, holding, daring, venturing, as we go, the unknown ways,
    Pioneers! O pioneers!

    We primeval forests felling,
We the rivers stemming, vexing we, and piercing deep the mines within;
We the surface broad surveying, we the virgin soil upheaving,
    Pioneers! O pioneers!

    Colorado men are we,
From the peaks gigantic, from the great sierras and the high plateaus,
From the mine and from the gully, from the hunting trail we come,
    Pioneers! O pioneers!

    From Nebraska, from Arkansas,
Central inland race are we, from Missouri, with the continental blood intervein'd;
All the hands of comrades clasping, all the Southern, all the Northern,
    Pioneers! O pioneers!

    O resistless, restless race!
O beloved race in all! O my breast aches with tender love for all!
O I mourn and yet exult—I am rapt with love for all,
    Pioneers! O pioneers!

    Raise the mighty mother mistress,
Waving high the delicate mistress, over all the starry mistress, (bend your heads all,)
Raise the fang'd and warlike mistress, stern, impassive, weapon'd mistress,
    Pioneers! O pioneers!

    See, my children, resolute children,
By those swarms upon our rear, we must never yield or falter,
Ages back in ghostly millions, frowning there behind us urging,
    Pioneers! O pioneers!

On and on, the compact ranks,
With accessions ever waiting, with the places of the dead quickly fill'd,
Through the battle, through defeat, moving yet and never stopping,
     Pioneers! O pioneers!

O to die advancing on!
Are there some of us to droop and die? has the hour come?
Then upon the march we fittest die, soon and sure the gap is fill'd,
     Pioneers! O pioneers!

All the pulses of the world,
Falling in, they beat for us, with the western movement beat;
Holding single or together, steady moving, to the front, all for us,
     Pioneers! O pioneers!

Life's involv'd and varied pageants,
All the forms and shows, all the workmen at their work,
All the seamen and the landsmen, all the masters with their slaves,
     Pioneers! O pioneers!

All the hapless silent lovers,
All the prisoners in the prisons, all the righteous and the wicked,
All the joyous, all the sorrowing, all the living, all the dying,
     Pioneers! O pioneers!

I too with my soul and body,
We, a curious trio, picking, wandering on our way,
Through these shores, amid the shadows, with the apparitions pressing,
     Pioneers! O pioneers!

Lo! the darting bowling orb!
Lo! the brother orbs around! all the clustering suns and planets,
All the dazzling days, all the mystic nights with dreams,
     Pioneers! O pioneers!

These are of us, they are with us,
All for primal needed work, while the followers there in embryo wait behind,
We to-day's procession heading, we the route for travel clearing,
    Pioneers! O pioneers!

    O you daughters of the west!
O you young and elder daughters! O you mothers and you wives!
Never must you be divided, in our ranks you move united,
    Pioneers! O pioneers!

    Minstrels latent on the prairies!
(Shrouded bards of other lands! you may sleep—you have done your work;)
Soon I hear you coming warbling, soon you rise and tramp amid us,
    Pioneers! O pioneers!

    Not for delectations sweet;
Not the cushion and the slipper, not the peaceful and the studious;
Not the riches safe and palling, not for us the tame enjoyment,
    Pioneers! O pioneers!

    Do the feasters gluttonous feast?
Do the corpulent sleepers sleep? have they lock'd and bolted doors?
Still be ours the diet hard, and the blanket on the ground,
    Pioneers! O pioneers!

    Has the night descended?
Was the road of late so toilsome? did we stop discouraged, nodding on our way?
Yet a passing hour I yield you, in your tracks to pause oblivious,
    Pioneers! O pioneers!

    Till with sound of trumpet,
Far, far off the day-break call—hark! how loud and clear I hear it wind;
Swift! to the head of the army!—swift! spring to your places,
    Pioneers! O pioneers.

SONG OF MYSELF, 6
(A CHILD SAID, WHAT IS THE GRASS?)

by *Walt Whitman*

A child said, What is the grass? fetching it to me with full
hands;
How could I answer the child?. . . .I do not know what it
is any more than he.

I guess it must be the flag of my disposition, out of hopeful
green stuff woven.

Or I guess it is the handkerchief of the Lord,
A scented gift and remembrancer designedly dropped,
Bearing the owner's name someway in the corners, that we
may see and remark, and say Whose?

Or I guess the grass is itself a child. . . .the produced babe
of the vegetation.

Or I guess it is a uniform hieroglyphic,
And it means, Sprouting alike in broad zones and narrow
zones,
Growing among black folks as among white,
Kanuck, Tuckahoe, Congressman, Cuff, I give them the
same, I receive them the same.

And now it seems to me the beautiful uncut hair of graves.

Tenderly will I use you curling grass,
It may be you transpire from the breasts of young men,
It may be if I had known them I would have loved them;
It may be you are from old people and from women, and
from offspring taken soon out of their mother's laps,
And here you are the mother's laps.

This grass is very dark to be from the white heads of old
mothers,
Darker than the colorless beards of old men,
Dark to come from under the faint red roofs of mouths.

O I perceive after all so many uttering tongues!
And I perceive they do not come from the roofs of mouths
for nothing.

I wish I could translate the hints about the dead young men
and women,
And the hints about old men and mothers, and the offspring
taken soon out of their laps.

What do you think has become of the young and old men?
What do you think has become of the women and
children?

They are alive and well somewhere;
The smallest sprouts show there is really no death,
And if ever there was it led forward life, and does not wait
at the end to arrest it,
And ceased the moment life appeared.

All goes onward and outward. . . .and nothing collapses,
And to die is different from what any one supposed, and
luckier.

MAUD MULLER

by John Greenleaf Whittier

Maud Muller, on a summer's day,
Raked the meadow sweet with hay.

Beneath her torn hat glowed the wealth
Of simple beauty and rustic health.

Singing, she wrought, and her merry glee
The mock-bird echoed from his tree.

But when she glanced to the far-off town,
White from its hill-slope looking down,

The sweet song died, and a vague unrest
And a nameless longing filled her breast,—

A wish that she hardly dared to own,
For something better than she had known.

The Judge rode slowly down the lane,
Smoothing his horse's chestnut mane.

He drew his bridle in the shade
Of the apple-trees to greet the maid,

And ask a draught from the spring that flowed
Through the meadow across the road.

She stooped where the cool spring bubbled up,
And filled for him her small tin cup,

And blushed as she gave it, looking down
On her feet so bare, and her tattered gown.
"Thanks!" said the Judge; "a sweeter draught
From a fairer hand was never quaffed."

He spoke of the grass and flowers and trees,
Of the singing birds and the humming bees;

Then talked of the haying, and wondered whether
The cloud in the west would bring foul weather.

And Maud forgot her brier-torn gown
And her graceful ankles bare and brown;

And listened, while a pleased surprise
Looked from her long-lashed hazel eyes.

At last, like one who for delay
Seeks a vain excuse, he rode away.

Maud Muller looked and sighed: "Ah me!
That I the Judge's bride might be!

"He would dress me up in silks so fine,
And praise and toast me at his wine.

"My father should wear a broadcloth coat;
My brother should sail a painted boat.

"I'd dress my mother so grand and gay,
And the baby should have a new toy each day.

"And I'd feed the hungry and clothe the poor,
And all should bless me who left our door."

The Judge looked back as he climbed the hill,
And saw Maud Muller standing still.

"A form more fair, a face more sweet,
Ne'er hath it been my lot to meet.

"And her modest answer and graceful air
Show her wise and good as she is fair.

"And her modest answer and graceful air
Show her wise and good as she is fair.

"No doubtful balance of rights and wrongs,
Nor weary lawyers with endless tongues,

"But low of cattle and song of birds,
And health and quiet and loving words."

But he thought of his sisters proud and cold,
And his mother vain of her rank and gold.

So, closing his heart, the Judge rode on,
And Maud was left in the field alone.

But the lawyers smiled that afternoon,
When he hummed in court an old love-tune;

And the young girl mused beside the well,
Till the rain on the unraked clover fell.

He wedded a wife of richest dower,
Who lived for fashion, as he for power.

Yet oft, in his marble hearth's bright glow,
He watched a picture come and go;

And sweet Maud Muller's hazel eyes
Looked out in their innocent surprise.

Oft, when the wine in his glass was red,
He longed for the wayside well instead;

And closed his eyes on his garnished rooms
To dream of meadows and clover-blooms.

And the proud man sighed, with a secret pain,
"Ah, that I were free again!

"Free as when I rode that day,
Where the barefoot maiden raked her hay."

She wedded a man unlearned and poor,
And many children played round her door.

But care and sorrow, and childbirth pain,
Left their traces on heart and brain.

And oft, when the summer sun shone hot
On the new-mown hay in the meadow lot,

And she heard the little spring brook fall
Over the roadside, through the wall,

In the shade of the apple-tree again
She saw a rider draw his rein.

And, gazing down with timid grace,
She felt his pleased eyes read her face.

Sometimes her narrow kitchen walls
Stretched away into stately halls;

The weary wheel to a spinet turned,
The tallow candle an astral burned,

And for him who sat by the chimney lug,
Dozing and grumbling o'er pipe and mug,

A manly form at her side she saw,
And joy was duty and love was law.

Then she took up her burden of life again,
Saying only, "It might have been."

Alas for maiden, alas for Judge,
For rich repiner and household drudge!

God pity them both! and pity us all,
Who vainly the dreams of youth recall.

For of all sad words of tongue or pen,
The saddest are these: "It might have been!"

Ah, well! for us all some sweet hope lies
Deeply buried from human eyes;

And, in the hereafter, angels may
Roll the stone from its grave away!

SNOW-BOUND

by John Greenleaf Whittier

The sun that brief December day
Rose cheerless over hills of gray,
And, darkly circled, gave at noon
A sadder light than waning moon.
Slow tracing down the thickening sky
Its mute and ominous prophecy,
A portent seeming less than threat,
It sank from sight before it set.
A chill no coat, however stout,
Of homespun stuff could quite shut out,
A hard, dull bitterness of cold,
     That checked, mid-vein, the circling race
     Of life-blood in the sharpened face,
The coming of the snow-storm told.
The wind blew east; we heard the roar
Of Ocean on his wintry shore,
And felt the strong pulse throbbing there
Beat with low rhythm our inland air.

Meanwhile we did our nightly chores,—
Brought in the wood from out of doors,
Littered the stalls, and from the mows
Raked down the herd's-grass for the cows;
Heard the horse whinnying for his corn;
And, sharply clashing horn on horn,
Impatient down the stanchion rows

The cattle shake their walnut bows;
While, peering from his early perch
Upon the scaffold's pole of birch,
The cock his crested helmet bent
And down his querulous challenge sent.

Unwarmed by any sunset light
The gray day darkened into night,
A night made hoary with the swarm
And whirl-dance of the blinding storm,
As zigzag, wavering to and fro,
Crossed and recrossed the wingéd snow:
And ere the early bedtime came
The white drift piled the window-frame,
And through the glass the clothes-line posts
Looked in like tall and sheeted ghosts.

So all night long the storm roared on:
The morning broke without a sun;
In tiny spherule traced with lines
Of Nature's geometric signs,
In starry flake, and pellicle,
All day the hoary meteor fell;
And, when the second morning shone,
We looked upon a world unknown,
On nothing we could call our own.
Around the glistening wonder bent
The blue walls of the firmament,
No cloud above, no earth below,—
A universe of sky and snow!
The old familiar sights of ours
Took marvellous shapes; strange domes and towers
Rose up where sty or corn-crib stood,
Or garden-wall, or belt of wood;
A smooth white mound the brush-pile showed,
A fenceless drift what once was road;
The bridle-post an old man sat

With loose-flung coat and high cocked hat;
The well-curb had a Chinese roof;
And even the long sweep, high aloof,
In its slant splendor, seemed to tell
Of Pisa's leaning miracle.

A prompt, decisive man, no breath
Our father wasted: "Boys, a path!"
Well pleased, (for when did farmer boy
Count such a summons less than joy?)
Our buskins on our feet we drew;
    With mittened hands, and caps drawn low,
    To guard our necks and ears from snow,
We cut the solid whiteness through.
And, where the drift was deepest, made
A tunnel walled and overlaid
With dazzling crystal: we had read
Of rare Aladdin's wondrous cave,
And to our own his name we gave,
With many a wish the luck were ours
To test his lamp's supernal powers.
We reached the barn with merry din,
And roused the prisoned brutes within.
The old horse thrust his long head out,
And grave with wonder gazed about;
The cock his lusty greeting said,
And forth his speckled harem led;
The oxen lashed their tails, and hooked,
And mild reproach of hunger looked;
The hornéd patriarch of the sheep,
Like Egypt's Amun roused from sleep,
Shook his sage head with gesture mute,
And emphasized with stamp of foot.

All day the gusty north-wind bore
The loosening drift its breath before;
Low circling round its southern zone,

The sun through dazzling snow-mist shone.
No church-bell lent its Christian tone
To the savage air, no social smoke
Curled over woods of snow-hung oak.
A solitude made more intense
By dreary-voicéd elements,
The shrieking of the mindless wind,
The moaning tree-boughs swaying blind,
And on the glass the unmeaning beat
Of ghostly finger-tips of sleet.
Beyond the circle of our hearth
No welcome sound of toil or mirth
Unbound the spell, and testified
Of human life and thought outside.
We minded that the sharpest ear
The buried brooklet could not hear,
The music of whose liquid lip
Had been to us companionship,
And, in our lonely life, had grown
To have an almost human tone.

As night drew on, and, from the crest
Of wooded knolls that ridged the west,
The sun, a snow-blown traveller, sank
From sight beneath the smothering bank,
We piled, with care, our nightly stack
Of wood against the chimney-back,—
The oaken log, green, huge, and thick,
And on its top the stout back-stick;
The knotty forestick laid apart,
And filled between with curious art
The ragged brush; then, hovering near,
We watched the first red blaze appear,
Heard the sharp crackle, caught the gleam
On whitewashed wall and sagging beam,
Until the old, rude-furnished room
Burst, flower-like, into rosy bloom;

While radiant with a mimic flame
Outside the sparkling drift became,
And through the bare-boughed lilac-tree
Our own warm hearth seemed blazing free.
The crane and pendent trammels showed,
The Turks' heads on the andirons glowed;
While childish fancy, prompt to tell
The meaning of the miracle,
Whispered the old rhyme: *"Under the tree,*
When fire outdoors burns merrily,
There the witches are making tea."

The moon above the eastern wood
Shone at its full; the hill-range stood
Transfigured in the silver flood,
Its blown snows flashing cold and keen,
Dead white, save where some sharp ravine
Took shadow, or the sombre green
Of hemlocks turned to pitchy black
Against the whiteness at their back.
For such a world and such a night
Most fitting that unwarming light,
Which only seemed where'er it fell
To make the coldness visible.

Shut in from all the world without,
We sat the clean-winged hearth about,
Content to let the north-wind roar
In baffled rage at pane and door,
While the red logs before us beat
The frost-line back with tropic heat;
And ever, when a louder blast
Shook beam and rafter as it passed,
The merrier up its roaring draught
The great throat of the chimney laughed;

The house-dog on his paws outspread
Laid to the fire his drowsy head,
The cat's dark silhouette on the wall
A couchant tiger's seemed to fall;
And, for the winter fireside meet,
Between the andirons' straddling feet,
The mug of cider simmered slow,
The apples sputtered in a row,
And, close at hand, the basket stood
With nuts from brown October's wood.

What matter how the night behaved?
What matter how the north-wind raved?
Blow high, blow low, not all its snow
Could quench our hearth-fire's ruddy glow.
O Time and Change!—with hair as gray
As was my sire's that winter day,
How strange it seems, with so much gone
Of life and love, to still live on!
Ah, brother! only I and thou
Are left of all that circle now,—
The dear home faces whereupon
That fitful firelight paled and shone.
Henceforward, listen as we will,
The voices of that hearth are still;
Look where we may, the wide earth o'er,
Those lighted faces smile no more.
We tread the paths their feet have worn,
    We sit beneath their orchard trees,
    We hear, like them, the hum of bees
And rustle of the bladed corn;
We turn the pages that they read,
    Their written words we linger o'er,
But in the sun they cast no shade,
No voice is heard, no sign is made,
    No step is on the conscious floor!

Yet Love will dream, and Faith will trust,
(Since He who knows our need is just,)
That somehow, somewhere, meet we must.
Alas for him who never sees
The stars shine through his cypress-trees!
Who, hopeless, lays his dead away,
Nor looks to see the breaking day
Across the mournful marbles play!
Who hath not learned, in hours of faith,
        The truth to flesh and sense unknown,
That Life is ever lord of Death,
        And Love can never lose its own!

We sped the time with stories old,
Wrought puzzles out, and riddles told,
Or stammered from our school-book lore
"The Chief of Gambia's golden shore."
How often since, when all the land
Was clay in Slavery's shaping hand,
As if a trumpet called, I've heard
Dame Mercy Warren's rousing word:
"Does not the voice of reason cry,
    Claim the first right which Nature gave,
From the red scourge of bondage to fly,
    Nor deign to live a burdened slave!"
Our father rode again his ride
On Memphremagog's wooded side;
Sat down again to moose and samp
In trapper's hut and Indian camp;
Lived o'er the old idyllic ease
Beneath St. François' hemlock-trees;
Again for him the moonlight shone
On Norman cap and bodiced zone;
Again he heard the violin play
Which led the village dance away.
And mingled in its merry whirl

The grandam and the laughing girl.
Or, nearer home, our steps he led
Where Salisbury's level marshes spread
    Mile-wide as flies the laden bee;
Where merry mowers, hale and strong,
Swept, scythe on scythe, their swaths along
    The low green prairies of the sea.
We shared the fishing off Boar's Head,
    And round the rocky Isles of Shoals
    The hake-broil on the drift-wood coals;
The chowder on the sand-beach made,
Dipped by the hungry, steaming hot,
With spoons of clam-shell from the pot.
We heard the tales of witchcraft old,
And dream and sign and marvel told
To sleepy listeners as they lay
Stretched idly on the salted hay,
Adrift along the winding shores,
When favoring breezes deigned to blow
The square sail of the gundelow
And idle lay the useless oars.

Our mother, while she turned her wheel
Or run the new-knit stocking-heel,
Told how the Indian hordes came down
At midnight on Concheco town,
And how her own great-uncle bore
His cruel scalp-mark to fourscore.
Recalling, in her fitting phrase,
    So rich and picturesque and free
    (The common unrhymed poetry
Of simple life and country ways,)
The story of her early days,—
She made us welcome to her home;

Old hearths grew wide to give us room;
We stole with her a frightened look
At the gray wizard's conjuring-book,
The fame whereof went far and wide
Through all the simple country side;
We heard the hawks at twilight play,
The boat-horn on Piscataqua,
The loon's weird laughter far away;
We fished her little trout-brook, knew
What flowers in wood and meadow grew,
What sunny hillsides autumn-brown
She climbed to shake the ripe nuts down,
Saw where in sheltered cove and bay,
The ducks' black squadron anchored lay,
And heard the wild-geese calling loud
Beneath the gray November cloud.

Then, haply, with a look more grave,
And soberer tone, some tale she gave
From painful Sewel's ancient tome,
Beloved in every Quaker home,
Of faith fire-winged by martyrdom,
Or Chalkley's Journal, old and quaint,—
Gentlest of skippers, rare sea-saint!—
Who, when the dreary calms prevailed,
And water-butt and bread-cask failed,
And cruel, hungry eyes pursued
His portly presence mad for food,
With dark hints muttered under breath
Of casting lots for life or death,
Offered, if Heaven withheld supplies,
To be himself the sacrifice.
Then, suddenly, as if to save
The good man from his living grave,
A ripple on the water grew,

A school of porpoise flashed in view.
"Take, eat," he said, "and be content;
These fishes in my stead are sent
By Him who gave the tangled ram
To spare the child of Abraham."

Our uncle, innocent of books,
Was rich in lore of fields and brooks,
The ancient teachers never dumb
Of Nature's unhoused lyceum.
In moons and tides and weather wise,
He read the clouds as prophecies,
And foul or fair could well divine,
By many an occult hint and sign,
Holding the cunning-warded keys
To all the woodcraft mysteries;
Himself to Nature's heart so near
That all her voices in his ear
Of beast or bird had meanings clear,
Like Apollonius of old,
Who knew the tales the sparrows told,
Or Hermes, who interpreted
What the sage cranes of Nilus said;
A simple, guileless, childlike man,
Content to live where life began;
Strong only on his native grounds,
The little world of sights and sounds
Whose girdle was the parish bounds,
Whereof his fondly partial pride
The common features magnified,
As Surrey hills to mountains grew
In White of Selborne's loving view,—
He told how teal and loon he shot,
And how the eagle's eggs he got,
The feats on pond and river done,
The prodigies of rod and gun;

Till, warming with the tales he told,
Forgotten was the outside cold,
The bitter wind unheeded blew,
From ripening corn the pigeons flew,
The partridge drummed i' the wood, the mink
Went fishing down the river-brink.
In fields with bean or clover gay,
The woodchuck, like a hermit gray,
    Peered from the doorway of his cell;
The muskrat plied the mason's trade,
And tier by tier his mud-walls laid;
And from the shagbark overhead
    The grizzled squirrel dropped his shell.

Next, the dear aunt, whose smile of cheer
And voice in dreams I see and hear,—
The sweetest woman ever Fate
Perverse denied a household mate,
Who, lonely, homeless, not the less
Found peace in love's unselfishness,
And welcome wheresoe'er she went,
A calm and gracious element,
Whose presence seemed the sweet income
And womanly atmosphere of home,—
Called up her girlhood memories,
The huskings and the apple-bees,
The sleigh-rides and the summer sails,
Weaving through all the poor details
And homespun warp of circumstance
A golden woof-thread of romance.
For well she kept her genial mood
And simple faith of maidenhood;
Before her still a cloud-land lay,
The mirage loomed across her way;
The morning dew, that dries so soon

With others, glistened at her noon;
Through years of toil and soil and care,
From glossy tress to thin gray hair,
All unprofaned she held apart
The virgin fancies of the heart.
Be shame to him of woman born
Who hath for such but thought of scorn.

There, too, our elder sister plied
Her evening task the stand beside;
A full, rich nature, free to trust,
Truthful and almost sternly just,
Impulsive, earnest, prompt to act,
And make her generous thought a fact,
Keeping with many a light disguise
The secret of self-sacrifice.
O heart sore-tried! thou hast the best
That Heaven itself could give thee,—rest,
Rest from all bitter thoughts and things!
　　How many a poor one's blessing went
　　With thee beneath the low green tent
Whose curtain never outward swings!

As one who held herself a part
Of all she saw, and let her heart
　　Against the household bosom lean,
Upon the motley-braided mat
Our youngest and our dearest sat,
Lifting her large, sweet, asking eyes,
　　Now bathed in the unfading green
And holy peace of Paradise.
Oh, looking from some heavenly hill,
　　Or from the shade of saintly palms,
　　Or silver reach of river calms,

Do those large eyes behold me still?
With me one little year ago:—
The chill weight of the winter snow
    For months upon her grave has lain;
And now, when summer south-winds blow
    And brier and harebell bloom again,
I tread the pleasant paths we trod,
I see the violet-sprinkled sod
Whereon she leaned, too frail and weak
The hillside flowers she loved to seek,
Yet following me where'er I went
With dark eyes full of love's content.
The birds are glad; the brier-rose fills
The air with sweetness; all the hills
Stretch green to June's unclouded sky;
But still I wait with ear and eye
For something gone which should be nigh,
A loss in all familiar things,
In flower that blooms, and bird that sings.
And yet, dear heart! remembering thee,
    Am I not richer than of old?
Safe in thy immortality,
    What change can reach the wealth I hold?
    What chance can mar the pearl and gold
Thy love hath left in trust with me?
And while in life's late afternoon,
    Where cool and long the shadows grow,
I walk to meet the night that soon
    Shall shape and shadow overflow,
I cannot feel that thou art far,
Since near at need the angels are;
And when the sunset gates unbar,
    Shall I not see thee waiting stand,
And, white against the evening star,
    The welcome of thy beckoning hand?

Brisk wielder of the birch and rule,
The master of the district school
Held at the fire his favored place,
Its warm glow lit a laughing face
Fresh-hued and fair, where scarce appeared
The uncertain prophecy of beard.
He teased the mitten-blinded cat,
Played cross-pins on my uncle's hat,
Sang songs, and told us what befalls
In classic Dartmouth's college halls.
Born the wild Northern hills among,
From whence his yeoman father wrung
By patient toil subsistence scant,
Not competence and yet not want,
He early gained the power to pay
His cheerful, self-reliant way;
Could doff at ease his scholar's gown
To peddle wares from town to town;
Or through the long vacation's reach
In lonely lowland districts teach,
Where all the droll experience found
At stranger hearths in boarding round,
The moonlit skater's keen delight,
The sleigh-drive through the frosty night,
The rustic party, with its rough
Accompaniment of blind-man's-buff,
And whirling-plate, and forfeits paid,
His winter task a pastime made.
Happy the snow-locked homes wherein
He tuned his merry violin,
Or played the athlete in the barn,
Or held the good dame's winding-yarn,
Or mirth-provoking versions told
Of classic legends rare and old,
Wherein the scenes of Greece and Rome

Had all the commonplace of home,
And little seemed at best the odds
'Twixt Yankee pedlers and old gods;
Where Pindus-born Arachthus took
The guise of any grist-mill brook,
And dread Olympus at his will
Became a huckleberry hill.

A careless boy that night he seemed;
    But at his desk he had the look
And air of one who wisely schemed,
    And hostage from the future took
    In trainéd thought and lore of book.
Large-brained, clear-eyed, of such as he
Shall Freedom's young apostles be,
Who, following in War's bloody trail,
Shall every lingering wrong assail;
All chains from limb and spirit strike,
Uplift the black and white alike;
Scatter before their swift advance
The darkness and the ignorance,
The pride, the lust, the squalid sloth,
Which nurtured Treason's monstrous growth,
Made murder pastime, and the hell
Of prison-torture possible;
The cruel lie of caste refute,
Old forms remould, and substitute
For Slavery's lash the freeman's will,
For blind routine, wise-handed skill;
A school-house plant on every hill,
Stretching in radiate nerve-lines thence
The quick wires of intelligence;
Till North and South together brought
Shall own the same electric thought,

In peace a common flag salute,
And, side by side in labor's free
And unresentful rivalry,
Harvest the fields wherein they fought.

Another guest that winter night
Flashed back from lustrous eyes the light.
Unmarked by time, and yet not young,
The honeyed music of her tongue
And words of meekness scarcely told
A nature passionate and bold,
Strong, self-concentred, spurning guide,
Its milder features dwarfed beside
Her unbent will's majestic pride.
She sat among us, at the best,
A not unfeared, half-welcome guest,
Rebuking with her cultured phrase
Our homeliness of words and ways.
A certain pard-like, treacherous grace
Swayed the lithe limbs and drooped the lash,
Lent the white teeth their dazzling flash;
And under low brows, black with night,
Rayed out at times a dangerous light;
The sharp heat-lightnings of her face
Presaging ill to him whom Fate
Condemned to share her love or hate.
A woman tropical, intense
In thought and act, in soul and sense,
She blended in a like degree
The vixen and the devotee,
Revealing with each freak or feint
     The temper of Petruchio's Kate,
The raptures of Siena's saint.
Her tapering hand and rounded wrist
Had facile power to form a fist;

The warm, dark languish of her eyes
Was never safe from wrath's surprise.
Brows saintly calm and lips devout
Knew every change of scowl and pout;
And the sweet voice had notes more high
And shrill for social battle-cry.

Since then what old cathedral town
Has missed her pilgrim staff and gown,
What convent-gate has held its lock
Against the challenge of her knock!
Through Smyrna's plague-hushed
thoroughfares,
Up sea-set Malta's rocky stairs,
Gray olive slopes of hills that hem
Thy tombs and shrines, Jerusalem,
Or startling on her desert throne
The crazy Queen of Lebanon
With claims fantastic as her own,
Her tireless feet have held their way;
And still, unrestful, bowed, and gray,
She watches under Eastern skies,
    With hope each day renewed and fresh,
    The Lord's quick coming in the flesh,
Whereof she dreams and prophesies!

Where'er her troubled path may be,
The Lord's sweet pity with her go!
The outward wayward life we see,
The hidden springs we may not know.
Nor is it given us to discern
What threads the fatal sisters spun,
Through what ancestral years has run
The sorrow with the woman born,
What forged her cruel chain of moods,
What set her feet in solitudes,
And held the love within her mute,

313

What mingled madness in the blood,
A life-long discord and annoy,
Water of tears with oil of joy,
And hid within the folded bud
    Perversities of flower and fruit.
It is not ours to separate
The tangled skein of will and fate,
To show what metes and bounds should stand
Upon the soul's debatable land,
And between choice and Providence
Divide the circle of events;
But He who knows our frame is just,
Merciful and compassionate,
And full of sweet assurances
And hope for all the language is,
That He remembereth we are dust!

At last the great logs, crumbling low,
Sent out a dull and duller glow,
The bull's-eye watch that hung in view,
Ticking its weary circuit through,
Pointed with mutely warning sign
Its black hand to the hour of nine.
That sign the pleasant circle broke:
My uncle ceased his pipe to smoke,
Knocked from its bowl the refuse gray,
And laid it tenderly away;
Then roused himself to safely cover
The dull red brands with ashes over.
And while, with care, our mother laid
The work aside, her steps she stayed
One moment, seeking to express
Her grateful sense of happiness
For food and shelter, warmth and health,
And love's contentment more than wealth,
With simple wishes (not the weak,
Vain prayers which no fulfilment seek,

But such as warm the generous heart,
O'er-prompt to do with Heaven its part)
That none might lack, that bitter night,
For bread and clothing, warmth and light.

Within our beds awhile we heard
The wind that round the gables roared,
With now and then a ruder shock,
Which made our very bedsteads rock.
We heard the loosened clapboards tost,
The board-nails snapping in the frost;
And on us, through the unplastered wall,
Felt the light sifted snow-flakes fall.
But sleep stole on, as sleep will do
When hearts are light and life is new;
Faint and more faint the murmurs grew,
Till in the summer-land of dreams
They softened to the sound of streams,
Low stir of leaves, and dip of oars,
And lapsing waves on quiet shores.

Next morn we wakened with the shout
Of merry voices high and clear;
And saw the teamsters drawing near
To break the drifted highways out.
Down the long hillside treading slow
We saw the half-buried oxen go,
Shaking the snow from heads uptost,
Their straining nostrils white with frost.
Before our door the straggling train
Drew up, an added team to gain.
The elders threshed their hands a-cold,
    Passed, with the cider-mug, their jokes
    From lip to lip; the younger folks
Down the loose snow-banks, wrestling, rolled,
Then toiled again the cavalcade

315

O'er windy hill, through clogged ravine,
　And woodland paths that wound between
Low drooping pine-boughs winter-weighed.
From every barn a team afoot,
At every house a new recruit,
Where, drawn by Nature's subtlest law,
Haply the watchful young men saw
Sweet doorway pictures of the curls
　And curious eyes of merry girls,
Lifting their hands in mock defence
Against the snow-ball's compliments,
And reading in each missive tost
The charm with Eden never lost.

We heard once more the sleigh-bells' sound;
And, following where the teamsters led,
The wise old Doctor went his round,
Just pausing at our door to say,
In the brief autocratic way
Of one who, prompt at Duty's call,
Was free to urge her claim on all,
　That some poor neighbor sick abed
At night our mother's aid would need.
For, one in generous thought and deed,
　What mattered in the sufferer's sight
　The Quaker matron's inward light,
The Doctor's mail of Calvin's creed?
All hearts confess the saints elect
　Who, twain in faith, in love agree,
And melt not in an acid sect
　The Christian pearl of charity!

So days went on: a week had passed
Since the great world was heard from last.
The Almanac we studied o'er,

Read and reread our little store
Of books and pamphlets, scarce a score;
One harmless novel, mostly hid
From younger eyes, a book forbid,
And poetry, (or good or bad,
A single book was all we had,)
Where Ellwood's meek, drab-skirted Muse,
    A stranger to the heathen Nine,
    Sang, with a somewhat nasal whine,
The wars of David and the Jews.
At last the floundering carrier bore
The village paper to our door.
Lo! broadening outward as we read,
To warmer zones the horizon spread
In panoramic length unrolled
We saw the marvels that it told.
Before us passed the painted Creeks,
    And daft McGregor on his raids
    In Costa Rica's everglades.
And up Taygetos winding slow
Rode Ypsilanti's Mainote Greeks,
A Turk's head at each saddle-bow!
Welcome to us its week-old news,
Its corner for the rustic Muse,
    Its monthly gauge of snow and rain,
Its record, mingling in a breath
The wedding bell and dirge of death:
Jest, anecdote, and love-lorn tale,
The latest culprit sent to jail;
Its hue and cry of stolen and lost,
Its vendue sales and goods at cost,
    And traffic calling loud for gain.
We felt the stir of hall and street,
The pulse of life that round us beat;
The chill embargo of the snow
Was melted in the genial glow;

Wide swung again our ice-locked door,
And all the world was ours once more!

Clasp, Angel of the backword look
    And folded wings of ashen gray
    And voice of echoes far away,
The brazen covers of thy book;
The weird palimpsest old and vast,
Wherein thou hid'st the spectral past;
Where, closely mingling, pale and glow
The characters of joy and woe;
The monographs of outlived years,
Or smile-illumed or dim with tears,
    Green hills of life that slope to death,
And haunts of home, whose vistaed trees
Shade off to mournful cypresses
    With the white amaranths underneath.
Even while I look, I can but heed
    The restless sands' incessant fall,
Importunate hours that hours succeed,
Each clamorous with its own sharp need,
    And duty keeping pace with all.
Shut down and clasp with heavy lids;
I hear again the voice that bids
The dreamer leave his dream midway
For larger hopes and graver fears:
Life greatens in these later years,
The century's aloe flowers to-day!

Yet, haply, in some lull of life,
Some Truce of God which breaks its strife,
The worldling's eyes shall gather dew,
    Dreaming in throngful city ways
Of winter joys his boyhood knew;
And dear and early friends—the few
Who yet remain—shall pause to view

These Flemish pictures of old days;
Sit with me by the homestead hearth,
And stretch the hands of memory forth
  To warm them at the wood-fire's blaze!
And thanks untraced to lips unknown
Shall greet me like the odors blown
From unseen meadows newly mown,
Or lilies floating in some pond,
Wood-fringed, the wayside gaze beyond;
The traveller owns the grateful sense
Of sweetness near, he knows not whence,
And, pausing, takes with forehead bare
The benediction of the air.

I LOVE YOU

by Ella Wheeler Wilcox

I love your lips when they're wet with wine
And red with a wild desire;
I love your eyes when the lovelight lies
Lit with a passionate fire.
I love your arms when the warm white flesh
Touches mine in a fond embrace;
I love your hair when the strands enmesh
Your kisses against my face.

Not for me the cold, calm kiss
Of a virgin's bloodless love;
Not for me the saint's white bliss,
Nor the heart of a spotless dove.
But give me the love that so freely gives
And laughs at the whole world's blame,
With your body so young and warm in my arms,
It sets my poor heart aflame.

So kiss me sweet with your warm wet mouth,
Still fragrant with ruby wine,
And say with a fervor born of the South
That your body and soul are mine.
Clasp me close in your warm young arms,
While the pale stars shine above,
And we'll live our whole young lives away
In the joys of a living love.

LIFE'S SCARS

by Ella Wheeler Wilcox

They say the world is round, and yet
I often think it square,
So many little hurts we get
From corners here and there.
But one great truth in life I've found,
While journeying to the West-
The only folks who really wound
Are those we love the best.

The man you thoroughly despise
Can rouse your wrath, 'tis true;
Annoyance in your heart will rise
At things mere strangers do;
But those are only passing ills;
This rule all lives will prove;
The rankling wound which aches and thrills
Is dealt by hands we love.

The choicest garb, the sweetest grace,
Are oft to strangers shown;
The careless mien, the frowning face,
Are given to our own.
We flatter those we scarcely know,
We please the fleeting guest,
And deal full many a thoughtless blow
To those who love us best.

Love does not grow on every tree,
Nor true hearts yearly bloom.
Alas for those who only see
This cut across a tomb!
But, soon or late, the fact grows plain
To all through sorrow's test:
The only folks who give us pain
Are those we love the best.

SOLITUDE

by Ella Wheeler Wilcox

Laugh, and the world laughs with you;
Weep, and you weep alone.
For the sad old earth must borrow its mirth,
But has trouble enough of its own.
Sing, and the hills will answer;
Sigh, it is lost on the air.
The echoes bound to a joyful sound,
But shrink from voicing care.

Rejoice, and men will seek you;
Grieve, and they turn and go.
They want full measure of all your pleasure,
But they do not need your woe.
Be glad, and your friends are many;
Be sad, and you lose them all.
There are none to decline your nectared wine,
But alone you must drink life's gall.

Feast, and your halls are crowded;
Fast, and the world goes by.
Succeed and give, and it helps you live,
But no man can help you die.
There is room in the halls of pleasure
For a long and lordly train,
But one by one we must all file on
Through the narrow aisles of pain.

HER VOICE

by Oscar Wilde

The wild bee reels from bough to bough
   With his furry coat and his gauzy wing.
Now in a lily-cup, and now
   Setting a jacinth bell a-swing,
      In his wandering;
Sit closer love: it was here I trow
      I made that vow,

Swore that two lives should be like one
   As long as the sea-gull loved the sea,
As long as the sunflower sought the sun,—
   It shall be, I said, for eternity
      'Twixt you and me!
Dear friend, those times are over and done.
      Love's web is spun.

Look upward where the poplar trees
   Sway in the summer air,
Here n the valley never a breeze
   Scatters the thistledown, but there
      Great winds blow fair
From the mighty murmuring mystical seas,
      And the wave-lashed leas.

Look upward where the white gull screams,
   What does it see that we do not see?
Is that a star? or the lamp that gleams
   On some outward voyaging argosy,—
      Ah! can it be
We have lived our lives in a land of dreams!
     How sad it seems.

Sweet, there is nothing left to say
   But this, that love is never lost,
Keen winter stabs the breasts of May
   Whose crimson roses burst his frost,
     Ships tempest-tossed
Will find a harbor in some bay,
     And so we may.

And there is nothing left to do
   But to kiss once again, and part,
Nay, there is nothing we should rue,
   I have my beauty,—you your Art,
     Nay, do not start,
One world was not enough for two
     Like me and you.

REQUIESCAT

by Oscar Wilde

Tread lightly, she is near
Under the snow,
Speak gently, she can hear
The daisies grow.

All her bright golden hair
Tarnished with rust,
She that was young and fair
Fallen to dust.

Lily-like, white as snow,
She hardly knew
She was a woman, so
Sweetly she grew.

Coffin-board, heavy stone,
Lie on her breast,
I vex my heart alone
She is at rest.

Peace, Peace, she cannot hear
Lyre or sonnet,
All my life's buried here,
Heap earth upon it.

SONNET TO LIBERTY

by Oscar Wilde

Not that I love thy children, whose dull eyes
See nothing save their own unlovely woe,
Whose minds know nothing, nothing care to know,—
But that the roar of thy Democracies,
Thy reigns of Terror, thy great Anarchies,
Mirror my wildest passions like the sea,—
And give my rage a brother——! Liberty!
For this sake only do thy dissonant cries
Delight my discreet soul, else might all kings
By bloody knout or treacherous cannonades
Rob nations of their rights inviolate
And I remain unmoved—and yet, and yet,
These Christs that die upon the barricades,
God knows it I am with them, in some things.

THE RED WHEELBARROW

by William Carlos Williams

so much depends
upon

a red wheel
barrow

glazed with rain
water

beside the white
chickens

DAFFODILS

by William Wordsworth

I wandered lonely as a cloud
That floats on high o'er vales and hills,
When all at once I saw a crowd,
A host, of golden daffodils;
Beside the lake, beneath the trees,
Fluttering and dancing in the breeze.

Continuous as the stars that shine
And twinkle on the milky way,
They stretched in never-ending line
Along the margin of a bay:
Ten thousand saw I at a glance,
Tossing their heads in sprightly dance.

The waves beside them danced; but they
Out-did the sparkling waves in glee:
A poet could not but be gay,
In such a jocund company:
I gazed—gazed—but little thought
What wealth the show to me had brought:

For oft, when on my couch I lie
In vacant or in pensive mood,
They flash upon that inward eye
Which is the bliss of solitude;
And then my heart with pleasure fills,
And dances with the daffodils.

THE WORLD IS TOO MUCH WITH US

by *William Wordsworth*

The world is too much with us; late and soon,
Getting and spending, we lay waste our powers;—
Little we see in Nature that is ours;
We have given our hearts away, a sordid boon!
This Sea that bares her bosom to the moon;
The winds that will be howling at all hours,
And are up-gathered now like sleeping flowers;
For this, for everything, we are out of tune;
It moves us not. Great God! I'd rather be
A Pagan suckled in a creed outworn;
So might I, standing on this pleasant lea,
Have glimpses that would make me less forlorn;
Have sight of Proteus rising from the sea;
Or hear old Triton blow his wreathèd horn.

MY HEART LEAPS UP

by *William Wordsworth*

My heart leaps up when I behold
  A rainbow in the sky:
So was it when my life began;
So is it now I am a man;
So be it when I shall grow old,
  Or let me die!
The Child is father of the Man;
And I could wish my days to be
Bound each to each by natural piety.

A SLUMBER DID MY SPIRIT SEAL

by William Wordsworth

A slumber did my spirit seal;
I had no human fears:
She seemed a thing that could not feel
The touch of earthly years.

No motion has she now, no force;
She neither hears nor sees;
Rolled round in earth's diurnal course,
With rocks, and stones, and trees.

THE SECOND COMING

by W.B. Yeats

Turning and turning in the widening gyre
The falcon cannot hear the falconer;
Things fall apart; the centre cannot hold;
Mere anarchy is loosed upon the world,
The blood-dimmed tide is loosed, and everywhere
The ceremony of innocence is drowned;
The best lack all conviction, while the worst
Are full of passionate intensity.

Surely some revelation is at hand;
Surely the Second Coming is at hand.
The Second Coming! Hardly are those words out
When a vast image out of *Spiritus Mundi*
Troubles my sight: somewhere in sands of the desert
A shape with lion body and the head of a man,
A gaze blank and pitiless as the sun,
Is moving its slow thighs, while all about it
Reel shadows of the indignant desert birds.
The darkness drops again; but now I know
That twenty centuries of stony sleep
Were vexed to nightmare by a rocking cradle,
And what rough beast, its hour come round at last,
Slouches towards Bethlehem to be born?

AEDH WISHES FOR THE CLOTHS OF HEAVEN

by W.B. Yeats

Had I the heavens' embroidered cloths,
Enwrought with golden and silver light,
The blue and the dim and the dark cloths
Of night and light and the half light,
I would spread the cloths under your feet:
But I, being poor, have only my dreams;
I have spread my dreams under your feet;
Tread softly because you tread on my dreams.

SAILING TO BYZANTIUM
by W.B. Yeats

That is no country for old men. The young
In one another's arms, birds in the trees
—Those dying generations—at their song,
The salmon-falls, the mackerel-crowded seas,
Fish, flesh, or fowl, commend all summer long
Whatever is begotten, born, and dies.
Caught in that sensual music all neglect
Monuments of unageing intellect.

An aged man is but a paltry thing,
A tattered coat upon a stick, unless
Soul clap its hands and sing, and louder sing
For every tatter in its mortal dress,
Nor is there singing school but studying
Monuments of its own magnificence;
And therefore I have sailed the seas and come
To the holy city of Byzantium.

O sages standing in God's holy fire
As in the gold mosaic of a wall,
Come from the holy fire, perne in a gyre,
And be the singing-masters of my soul.
Consume my heart away; sick with desire
And fastened to a dying animal
It knows not what it is; and gather me
Into the artifice of eternity.

Once out of nature I shall never take
My bodily form from any natural thing,
But such a form as Grecian goldsmiths make
Of hammered gold and gold enamelling
To keep a drowsy Emperor awake;
Or set upon a golden bough to sing
To lords and ladies of Byzantium
Of what is past, or passing, or to come.

Made in the USA
Las Vegas, NV
12 March 2023

68930359R00203